INVESTIGATIVE INTERVIEWER'S GUIDEBOOK

Paul Starrett, J.D.

This book is an instructional adaptation of a compilation of Interview and Interrogation and The Dynamics of Eyewitness Testimony, which are copyrighted by Paul Starrett.

This First version of this text was published under the title: INTERVIEW & INTERROGATION with EYEWITNESS EVIDENCE. It contains the same subject matter, but with content clarification in various areas by the author, and retains its original learning goals and objectives.

Hardcover ISBN: 978-0-911983-05-0

ABOUT THE AUTHOR

Paul Starrett is a licensed private investigator and attorney in the state of California. He has been nationally published since 1998 in the areas of interview and interrogations, eyewitness evidence and other investigations titles. He has been formally trained in the area of investigative interviewing and, with this training, he has conducted thousands of interview and interrogations over a period of decades on large and complex matters.

He has over 30 years of experience in the security industry, with 12 years in corporate security, 4 years of experience in law enforcement, and 5 years as an information-security engineer.

He currently handles investigations that involve complex legal and technical issues.

CONTENTS

INTRODUCTION

Investigators utilize many tools and resources to gather evidence for their cases and research. One such resource, which is the most valuable, is also the most complex—the human being. And, the tools investigators use for this resource consist of interview and interrogation skills. This book was designed, organized, and written to address this very unique, challenging, and indispensable source of information.

This book is split into two parts followed by two appendices. In fact, each "part" originally consisted of a standalone book, one on interview and interrogation and the other on eyewitness evidence. These two books were combined into one to provide a single reference—the only one of its kind. The two-part approach begins, in part one, with the basic interview. The interview is the foundation upon which other skills are developed. Also, the interview is typically used at the beginning of a case or in the initial phases of research. Interrogation naturally flows from the interview chapters in part one to complete the skill sets needed to extract and distill the needed information effectively.

What makes this book unique is the attention given to the subject of eyewitness evidence. This area of forensics is an interesting mix of psychology, law, and specialized interview techniques. To properly address this important topic, it was necessary to devote the entire second part to it. Given its unique subject matter, it does not easily flow with the other subjects, i.e., interviews and interrogation. The net result, however, is a complete, robust, and thorough resource.

Finally, an investigator is better able to probe for relevant information and evidence when their legal and technical skills are properly developed and honed. We include an appendix devoted to each topic. In Appendix A, we address technical avenues, both from a topical standpoint and a learning method approach. In Appendix B, we present the same information but for learning legal principles and regulatory frameworks. Armed with these additional skills, you will be able to reflexively inquire about relevant avenues when you are interviewing anyone.

NOTE: We will use third-person, singular to discuss others in this text. Rather than using "he or she," we will use "he" for the sake of simplicity. No preference for one gender or another should be implied.

PART 1.

INTERVIEW AND INTERROGATION

CHAPTER 1.

INTRODUCTION TO INTERVIEW AND INTERROGATION

CHAPTER OVERVIEW

Interviews and interrogations are the beginning or backbone of an investigation, whether it is a criminal act, a breach of contract, a tort, or a compliance/ regulatory issue. Therefore, it is important to understand not only the history of interviews and interrogations but also the basic definitions, skills, different types of interviews, and legal constraints.

OBJECTIVES

To teach the reader how to...

- Define the terms Interview, Interrogation, Admission, and Confession.
- Identify the three ways to acquire the necessary interviewer skills.
- Define the differences and similarities between public and private sector interviews.
- Define the reason a firm legal foundation is necessary before conducting interviews.

A HISTORICAL PERSPECTIVE

The process of interview and interrogation is both an art and a science. As an art, it involves ingenuity and creativity. As a science, it involves careful preparation, following an established method, collecting and classifying information, reaching a conclusion, and verification, of the results.

It hasn't always been this way. In ancient times, the accused didn't have the benefit of a constitution that presumes innocence. In fact, in most cases, the opposite was true, and the accused was presumed guilty and had to prove his innocence. Civil and criminal law had yet to be separated. To further complicate the dilemma of an accused person, religious law formed a core ingredient in the process, there being no separation of religion or church and state at that time. This mixture of ecclesiastical, civil, and criminal law created a climate in which the survival of the accused was definitely an issue in doubt.

A great deal of creativity went into the development of apparatus and methods of extracting the "truth". Inquisitors of various types burned, stretched, sliced, smashed, and beat poor unfortunates as a way of helping them cleanse their souls and consciences of evil and confess to the crime they were accused of committing. Many of these offenses are not considered crimes today. For example, just a few hundred years ago, being an adulterer or a pickpocket could lead to a hanging. An epileptic seizure might be considered "witch-like" behavior, landing the poor soul at the feet of the authorities with torture and death as a possible end result. Even if one confessed, they were usually dispatched to their maker with a clean slate.

Time marched on and the precursors of the present criminal justice system were being developed. It still wasn't until fairly recently that violent interrogations were gradually eliminated by statute and case law in response to changes in public attitude. Sadly, in many third-world countries, physical abuse and torture are still used as interrogative methods.

The days of the bright light and the rubber hose have been replaced by skilled interviewers and interrogators using the "art and science" of today to glean the truth.

DEFINITIONS

Interview

The process of seeking, obtaining, and evaluating information from someone with knowledge of circumstances or events

As an interview runs its course, the information obtained may, depending on the case, heighten suspicion on the part of the interviewer to the point when the interviewer becomes the interrogator. This leads us to the next definition.

Interrogation

The questioning of an individual suspected of the issues, liability, or culpability of the investigation.

There is a definite distinction between these two closely related processes, i.e. , interview and interrogation. In this part of the book, you may find that some approaches used in interviews and interrogations are quite similar, while others are quite different. An interrogation, though, is merely another form of fact-gathering. It is more of a negotiation and exploration of facts, involvement, and responsibility for the target issues in the investigation. As stated at the outset of this book, the modern "interrogation," despite its colloquial negative connotations, is a fair and measured exploration to get to the truth.

Within this field, there are two other terms with similar sounding names and different definitions, which are usually the object of investigative efforts. They are admission and confession. As mentioned above, the following definitions are normally relevant.

Admission

An admission is a voluntary acknowledgment of, or a statement of facts, without an acknowledgment of liability or culpability.

This is not as complicated as it sounds. It merely means that an individual is revealing what they have knowledge of or may have been involved in an incident. In an admission, guilt may be inferred, but the acknowledgment is short of a confession of guilt.

Confession

A voluntary statement made acknowledging responsibility for some culpability or liability.

"I did it". This is a complete avowal of "guilt" with no inference to the contrary.

Can it happen today?

January 21, 1998, Escondido, CA–Twelve-year-old Stephanie Crowe was found stabbed to death in her bedroom in this San Diego suburb. Five family members were in the home; her parents, grandmother, sister, and brother, and told police they didn't hear any sounds of a struggle. Police interviewed and interrogated her older brother, and then arrested Michael Crowe, and two of his friends for murdering his younger sister by stabbing her nine times. Police based the arrest on Michael Crowe's, and his accomplices' videotaped confessions.

It sounds like a terrible crime, committed for whatever reason, that police were able to solve quickly through interrogation of the subjects. But that may not be the case. The day before the juvenile defendants were to go to trial, DNA evidence found Stephanie's blood on the clothing of a 33-year-old mentally ill homeless man seen in the neighborhood the night of her murder. The juvenile's attorney brought in interview and interrogation experts that reviewed hours of the videotaped interrogations and then testified that the defendants had been coerced into confessing to a crime they didn't commit. Media reports and experts have heavily criticized the techniques used by the detectives. The juveniles were not allowed to see or speak to their parents, an attorney, or any other adult. They were also deprived of food, sleep, and bathroom breaks during sessions lasting up to 12 hours. All charges were dismissed against all three defendants.

So, while beginning the study of interviewing and interrogation, one must keep the Crowe case in mind. Legal, ethical, and moral rules govern those entrusted with seeking the truth.

ACQUISITION OF SKILLS

While innate skills play some role, there's no such thing as a person who is "born" an interviewer or interrogator. The necessary skills must, ultimately, be acquired. Reading this part of the book and retaining the information contained within opens the door for the acquisition of skills or the honing of existing skills, as an interviewer and an interrogator.

Knowledge and concepts gained from this part of the book must then be applied to the real world of the investigator. There are a couple of ways in which to do this.

Observation

One way is to closely observe an experienced and successful investigator. The emphasis is on "successful". Not everyone with many years on the job is necessarily good at interviewing and interrogating. If you watch and listen, you will see that the book comes alive as the information read about and labeled suddenly becomes clear. The terms and definitions will have real meaning.

Academic

The other way is, as they say, academic. You can watch investigators for hours as they question subjects, but without a firm academic foundation, you will never achieve a full understanding of the dynamics of the art and science of interview and interrogation. At this point in history, on-the-job training is just not sufficient, so read on.

Combining The Two — Observations and Academics

To do the best possible job as an interviewer or interrogator, observation and academic methods must be combined to form a well-rounded professional.

As a relatively new and inexperienced investigator, in either the private or public sector, you will be given relatively minor cases under supervision to cut your teeth on. The risk is minimal and the learning quotient is maximized. Regardless of whether the incident is a shoplifting case, a tortious act, a contract breach, or a violation of other law, the basic concepts are the same... getting to the truth by asking questions.

THE PUBLIC AND PRIVATE SECTORS

Interviews and interrogations are conducted both in the public and private sectors, with some marked differences.

Public Sector

The public sector is primarily composed of governmental agencies, with an emphasis on the prosecution of people accused of crimes, civil actions, or other violations of law. Also within the public sector is the defense. Often it is the public defender's office that employs investigators who primarily conduct interviews in an effort to exonerate their clients.

One obvious concern within the public sector is the law as it applies to search and seizure, arrest and detention, entrapment, the Miranda rule, and other court cases related to interview and interrogation. It is incumbent on the interviewer or interrogator to be familiar with the law as it applies to a given jurisdiction. If in doubt, seek legal counsel.

Private Sector

Generally composed of private investigators, private industry investigators, auditors, risk professionals and other non-governmental agencies, the private sector has much broader interests. The issues may be to have a person removed from employment, to obtain restitution for some wrong, and/or for criminal investigations. Frequently, criminal defense teams hire private investigators, so the two sectors do sometimes overlap in the scope of their interests.

Again, the law is much different as it applies in the private sector, where there is limited authority but sometimes fewer constitutional roadblocks. Privacy issues, searches by civilians, and detentions are but a few of the legal concerns faced by investigators in the private sector. Again, it is advised to be familiar with the law.

LEGAL CONCERNS

All agencies, whether public or private, will have different values and priorities. The application of the law is very different. Issues are particularly vexing in the areas of harassment, discrimination, retaliation, privacy, and confidentiality. How this concerns an investigation is not something that this book covers in any particular depth or breadth. Before applying the methods explained in this book, the readers should have a firm legal foundation within their given profession and, if questions arise, should consult their superiors or appropriate legal counsel before compromising an investigation.

Incrimination and Miranda

"Read him his rights and book him." Sound familiar? That line is heard often in TV shows and movies. But what does it really mean? The Miranda warning comes from Miranda v. Arizona 384 U.S. 436 (1966). The basic facts of the case are that $8.00 was stolen from a victim on March 13, 1963, and the police later arrested Ernesto Miranda for the crime. Mr. Miranda was interrogated for approximately 2 hours, finally confessing to the crime of theft and also to unrelated crimes of kidnapping and rape of a woman several days earlier. Mr. Miranda was never offered the services of a lawyer.

Mr. Miranda was convicted, based partly on his confession, and was sentenced to twenty years in prison. The United States Supreme Court reversed the ruling of the Arizona Supreme Court and ordered a new trial at which his confession could not be used as evidence...the "Miranda" warning was established.

The importance of conducting legal interviews and interrogations cannot be stressed enough. This book provides the you with techniques and skills to become effective interviewers/interrogators. Practitioners must seek competent legal advice and remain current on all appropriate legal updates.

Side Point: Mr. Miranda was convicted of kidnap and rape in his second trial, even without his confession, and was paroled in 1972 after serving 11 years.

Final Note: Mr. Miranda was stabbed to death in a fight in 1976. The suspected assailant invoked his Miranda rights (remained silent) when interrogated by the police, and was released.

Interviews are replete with legal issues. This book cannot cover all of them, nor with any particular depth. However, many of the more common issues relate to:

Privacy laws / Confidentiality

These laws may dictate what information an investigator can seek from an individual and what can be recorded or shared. As you perform research or conduct other investigations, be aware of recent laws limit what kind of information can be gathered from a database or a record unless they have consent or some other justification. If the topic is confidential, the investigator must ensure that the discussions are with those who need to know and that no one can overhear their conversations. Heed these issues in your communications and written reports.

Workplace investigations

Workplace investigations often involve violations of state or federal disability, discrimination, and retaliation laws. Special, in-depth training is often necessary or required. For example, an Upjohn warning may need to be given if an attorney is performing an interview. The attorney must let the subject know that they are not their client and that a third-party or an enterprise is their client. This is so that the subject is not confused in believing that the interviewer is their attorney and that the interview with the subject is covered by the attorney-client privilege.

False imprisonment

This theory may be alleged if the person being interviewed does not feel they are free to leave the interview environment. This is a somewhat subjective standard and one that is contextual. For example, it may not be a good idea to stand between the subject and the door to a room or to corner the subject into one part of the room.

Defamation

When one asserts a fact as true that is not true, and this is communicated to a third party and causes damage, one could be on the hook for damages that result from this. Generally, defamation is: 1) a false statement purporting to be fact (not opinion); 2) negligently or intentionally published or communicated to a third person; and 3) damages (damages can be assumed in some cases). Defamation comes in two forms: libel, which is in written form, and slander, which is in spoken or verbal form.

For example, if John says that Paul is a criminal, and he is not (an untrue fact) and this is negligently or intentionally communicated to a third party, this is defamation. Truth is often a complete defense to defamation. Of course, not every false assertion of fact will result in "damage." The analysis is contextual and open to argument. So, be careful about drawing conclusions and what is communicated to others and what is put in the reports during an investigation.

These are a smattering of the issues. Again, check with a relevant legal professional as needed.

SUMMARY

The technical skills necessary to conduct a successful interview or interrogation are only part of the process to determine the truth. Legal, ethical, and moral considerations play an equally important part.

CHAPTER 2.

COMMUNICATIONS THEORY

CHAPTER OVERVIEW

A great deal of time is spent communicating on various levels and for various purposes. Until you start communicating with a mission in mind, you won't necessarily look at the process from a theoretical viewpoint. Communications theory is another important component in having a complete understanding of the interview and interrogation process. The need to know this information is obvious. Much of it is common sense and common knowledge but is often forgotten during interviews. Many of the concepts taught in this section will be referred to in later sections of the book.

OBJECTIVES

To teach the reader how to...

- Identify how information is lost during communication.
- Identify four common distractions to communication.
- Identify how vocabulary can affect the communication process.
- Define "the unstated assumption".
- Explain "schemas" in the communication process.
- Identify how cultural differences can affect the communications process.
- Define the three modes of speech.

INTRODUCTION

Communications theory refers to assumptions about how and why humans communicate. The American Heritage College Dictionary defines communica-

tion as the exchange of thoughts, messages, or information. It is the transfer of ideas or information from one person to another. In order to understand communications theory, you must understand the reasons for communication. Generally, people communicate for four reasons: to provide adequate information for group living, to clarify perceptions and expectations, to stimulate creative thinking, and to maintain balance in the world. Communication may occur in a variety of ways: a spoken language or dialect, a stone inscription, a Morse code signal, or a chain of binary numbers in a computer, etc. Inherent in the act of communication is the transmission and receipt of a message to affect some kind of action. However, many times in a society this transmission of information is interrupted for a number of reasons.

The process of communication can be diagrammed in the Sender-Receiver-Feedback loop. The sender (speaker) sends information to the receiver (listener), the receiver receives the information, and as a result, the receiver sends feedback to the sender regarding what was communicated. For the purposes of this book, the words sender and speaker, and receiver and listener will be used interchangeably.

Communication requires two people; a speaker and a listener. It is the speaker's responsibility to send clear, complete messages, and monitor feedback to ensure the message was accurately communicated. It is the listener's responsibility to receive the information and then provide feedback about what was received. A good way to do this is to use reflective listening. Reflective listening is when the listener reflects on what the subject heard the speaker say.

Reflective listening ensures the listener correctly heard what the speaker said. It also helps the listener filter out any biases or inferences the subject may have unconsciously made. Furthermore, it gives the speaker the opportunity to hear what the subject said and make corrections if necessary. Reflective listening also ensures that the listener has heard everything the speaker said. Frequently complications occur which cause the listener to miss some of the information the speaker is trying to convey. This can be thought of as lost information. Lost information refers to information the speaker thinks they sent, but the listener did not receive. It can be compared to a leaking water pipe. If the speaker sends A and B leaks out, A minus B is what was communicated. In order to avoid leakage, the speaker and listener can use reflective listening. Leakage can also be avoided when the speaker is aware of factors that can hinder communication.

DISTRACTIONS

Distractions can impede effective communication. They can take several forms, including environmental stimuli, emotional stress, internal stress, and attention span. Environmental distractions are competing stimuli like noise, visual distractions, and extreme temperatures. These stimuli can make it difficult for the listener to focus on the sender. Modifying the environment to reduce the stimuli can easily reduce this type of distraction. Other distractions, like emotional and internal stress, are not as easily addressed.

Emotional Stress

Emotional stress is the result of a lack of physical or mental relaxation. This occurs when a subject is responding emotionally to their current situation. Addressing the subject's symptoms can alleviate emotional stress. For example, if the subject exhibits symptoms of anger, ask why the subject is angry. Environmental factors such as temperature, humidity, noise, and glare can affect a person's emotional stress. If emotion is witnessed, you must be do what you can to lessen anything in the environment that might exacerbate this state. Emotional stress can cause the person to exaggerate the message the subject received. Therefore, it is important to be cognizant of exaggeration or over-generalization of what you are saying to a person who is emotional. Issues associated with emotions will be addressed in greater detail in Chapter Three: Psychological Issues.

Internal Stress

Another type of distraction that can interfere with communication is internal stress. Internal stress refers to stress that is generated from internal stimuli rather than external stimuli. Internal stress can result from lack of sleep, poor health, drugs, sensory deprivation, and mood variations. All of these factors can affect the reception of information. Evidence of internal stress may include exaggeration or overconfidence in the subject's communication being properly received. If such symptoms are observed, you must inquire about factors that can create internal stress and modify the interview as necessary.

Attention Span

Attention span is an additional distraction that can impede communication. Attention span is the amount of time an individual can remain focused on a given topic. Proceeding too slowly or too quickly can either exceed or bog down an individual's capacity to concentrate. It is important to be aware of the subject's attention span. If the subject appears to be losing interest, it may be due to his attention span, and you will need to modify the interview accordingly.

VOCABULARY

The use of unfamiliar vocabulary is another factor that can inhibit communication. This may include primary language problems, such as dialect or language fluency, the use of jargon, or the use of "big" words. It is important to establish the subject's primary language and typical vocabulary during the early part of the interview.

It is also helpful to determine the subject's level of education and occupation. Special consideration should be given to the use of slang, jargon, "deadwood words," shop talk, and euphemisms. You may or may not want to use them.

Slang is an inappropriate street language that a person may or may not understand. Jargon is the specialized language of a profession, such as undefined penal code sections and radio codes. "Deadwood words" are fancy, formal, or grand expressions that may not be useful to the interviewer.

A euphemism is a polite or diplomatic way to say something that might otherwise be taken as an insult or uncomplimentary remark. In general, it is wise to use common, everyday words in the questions and comments. The effect of the investigator's language will be discussed further in Chapter Five: The Interrogation Preparation Phase.

Examples of Slang or Jargon:

- Contacted – called, talked to
- Stated – said, told me

- Observed – saw
- Exit, exited – leave, left
- Negative results – empty, couldn't find
- It should be noted that – furthermore

Examples of Deadwood Words:

- Accomplish, execute, perform – do
- Acquire, secure – get
- Despite the fact that – although
- During the time that - while

Examples of Euphemisms:

- Penis – private parts
- Bra and panties – under-garments
- Used – previously owned car
- Obese – weight issue

UNSTATED ASSUMPTIONS

Unstated assumptions can also hinder communication. An unstated assumption is a presumption the speaker makes without verbally expressing it to the listener. For example, when giving a narrative account of the incident in question, the subject says they were carrying an umbrella, and the interviewer makes the unstated assumption that it was raining. It may or may not have been raining. The interviewer assumed it was raining because the subject recalled carrying an umbrella. An unstated assumption may be a word, sentence, phrase, or an entire area of a discussion.

In this type of situation, it is important to be aware of catch phrases and ready-made opinions. On the receiving end, the receiver may think that their inability to understand is due to their own ignorance rather than the fact that the deliverer did not convey enough information. When this occurs, the receiver may be too embarrassed to ask for clarification. It can also be that the deliverer does not want to bore the receiver with what the subject feels the receiver already knows.

SCHEMAS

Schemas are a way of organizing information based on past experience. It is how the brain makes sense of what is seen and heard. A person cannot take in all they see and hear, therefore, the mind organizes this information into schemas. These are simplified versions of information the brain receives. As such, a person will have the illusion they are taking in reality, but really the brain is processing the information in relation to previous information. New information is constantly related to old information stored in human's memory. This past information and experience predisposes how a person perceives and behaves. Schemas are used in learning and adaptation. Schemas exist throughout every aspect of life. People have schemas for smell, touch, and taste, while others are for social, religious, family, sex, nationality, economic experiences as well as other behaviors. Generally, people are unaware of their schemas.

So why are schemas important? People comprehend or derive meaning based on their schemas. This is true for both the speaker and the listener in the communication process. A listener may misinterpret a speaker's message based on his own schema. People do not want to face or believe anything that challenges an existing schema. They make assessments based on how information measures up to what is currently in their bank of schemas. So, the importance of the schema is that it is at the very core of the thought process, and as such, in the communication and interpretation process.

One type of schema most lay people are familiar with is the stereotype. Stereotypes are created as a way of organizing information about people. As mentioned previously, they are created based on one's past experiences. People not only tend to stereotype others but also themselves. Stereotypes are not inherently bad; they are necessary to organize individuals into separate and clear functions. Formalized roles such as parent, child, spouse, and employer are stereotypes. Everyone has their own schema to define these stereotypes. To help illustrate this concept, visualize a speaker in a room alone. Then imagine gradually introducing different people into the room. Imagine how the speaker would communicate with other people. They would communicate differently with each person based on their schemas. It is important to consider how schema can affect an interview.

CULTURAL DIFFERENCES

Cultural differences can impede communication when the speaker and listener are from cultures with differing methods of communication. For example, in any culture, people use eye contact as a means of showing attention, while avoiding eye contact is viewed as a sign of deception or disrespect. However, in some cultures, direct eye contact is a sign of disrespect. It is important for you to recognize when there is a conflict in cultural communication style and interpret it correctly. It is your responsibility to determine when conflicting communication styles are the result of cultural differences or manipulative behavior.

MODES OF SPEECH

Modes of speech refer to a person's style of communicating. A person has a dominant speech mode in visual, auditory, or kinetic communicative methods.

Visual

Visual people communicate visually; they form pictures with their words. They speak to convey images, like describing something as a picture, such as "I see what you are saying," "Look at it this way," "See if you can tell," and "Let me give you a picture." These people speak quickly and in a raised tone. They also tend to breathe high in the chest. These people may appear to reenact the event as they talk about it in an effort to recreate it visually.

Auditory

Auditory people express what they hear, thinking more in terms such as "I hear you," "Listen closely," "It sounds to me like," etc. These people breathe from the entire chest area and have a steady and clear speech. This mode is also common with people who are shy.

Kinetic

Kinetic people express themselves based on feeling or emotion and might use phrases like, "How do you feel about this?" or "Do you feel what I feel?" "Can you get in touch with my meaning?" These people generally speak in a deep and slow voice and tend to breathe from the stomach. They tend to use expressive gestures that communicate feeling.

To help build rapport, you should mirror what mode the subject is in. If the person is kinetic, say, "Let's get a grip on what is happening here," or "I feel where you are coming from." With an auditory person use similar language that they will respond to, "Listen to me," "I hear you," etc. With visual people use, "I see what you're saying," and "Help me form a picture." You increase the subject's attention and communication with him.

SUMMARY

A thorough understanding of communications theory is an essential building block in the interview and interrogation process, and you have to have it before actually asking questions. People are all different, yet there are many similarities based on situations and circumstances. It is much easier to get the information you want when you understand where the other person is coming from.

DISCUSSION QUESTIONS

- What distractions can you think of just sitting where you are?
- What other types or causes of emotional stress can you think of?
- What other types or causes of internal stress can you think of?
- Why are schemas important in communications theory?

CHAPTER 3.

PSYCHOLOGICAL ISSUES

CHAPTER OVERVIEW

An interview is an interaction between people. By understanding the overall psychological issues that can affect the interview process, you will be more effective in getting important information. Some of these psychological issues include basic personality types, perceptions, emotions, and interpersonal skills. This information can also be useful in helping the interviewer plan, manage, and focus on the interview.

Note that this section contains some overlap of information. For example, interpersonal skills always involve some communication skills and vice versa. For each subject to make sense, though, each needs to be presented separately, as though it was being read by itself. You will come away with a broad and complete understanding of the content as a whole.

OBJECTIVES

To teach the reader how to...

- Define the three interpersonal orientations personality types.
- Define the three problem-solving personality types.
- Identify characteristics common to interviewing children, adolescents and young adults, adults, and the elderly.
- Explain the importance of perception, emotion, and persuasion in the interview process.

BASIC PERSONALITY TYPES

There are two standard classifications of basic personality types: interpersonal orientations and problem-solving. The interpersonal orientations classification considers the specifics of human interaction. The problem-solving classification deals more with how different people approach a problem. Understanding the basic personality type of the person being interviewed is essential to help get what one needs.

Interpersonal Orientations Personality Type

The interpersonal orientations classification considers how a person interacts with others. These personality types may seem similar to the problem-solving personality types and, to some extent, there is overlap. But they are distinct in that they determine more specifically the dynamics that occur between two people. The interpersonal orientations personality types are:

Control - These people like to exert control over others, to take charge,

Inclusion - These people want to join groups and be around other people,

Affection - These people like close and personal relationships.

In an interview situation, you and the person being interviewed may be of conflicting types. For example, if both are the "control" type, they may clash or if one is outgoing (inclusion) and another is more introverted (affection), there may be an uncomfortable atmosphere. During an interview, you should use the subject's personality type to your advantage. For example, if the person is outgoing (inclusion), approach him as a team player in the interview. Emphasizing growth and competition should yield a lot of feedback from this person. If the person is introverted (affection), you should discuss his importance as a person and how the he is appreciated. If the person is the control type, let him control the interview to a certain extent.

No one person is exclusively one or the other; there will be some mix. However, a person is more likely to be one more than the other. Use common sense.

Problem-Solving Personality

There are three different types of problem-solving personalities. Although everybody has some combination of each, one will be dominant. Problem-solving personality types are distinct from the interpersonal orientations personality types mentioned above (control, inclusion, affection). Problem-solving personality types consider how a person approaches a problem rather than the direct interaction between two people. Obviously, there is overlap. The problem-solving personality types are:

The task-oriented person - This person is detail oriented and analytical but may miss the big picture. They are meticulous. They need security in a predictable and stable world and may view you as a nitpicker as you probe for specific information in an interview.

Goal-oriented person - This person is concerned about the bottom line and, in contrast to the task-oriented person, they do see the big picture. They are direct, but they tend to miss details. They exude authority and status and are proud and decisive. These people can be impatient and insensitive.

People-oriented person - This person is accepting, compassionate, and helpful. They need to feel loved and as though they belong. Their problem is they try to be all things to all people and as such waiver and generally stay unfocused.

The best person to be in an interview is the first person, the task-oriented person. This is the frame of mind that gets the facts with the least amount of effort and tends to put others at ease. There may be times when you will need to become other types. For example, become a goal-oriented person if the interviewee gets out of line or strays from the subject. Or, if the person is upset, fearful, or otherwise reluctant, perhaps the people-oriented type is most appropriate. Your flexibility with these "personalities" will help you get a better interview and have more control over it.

AGE ISSUES

Subjects differ greatly in their responses during an interview or interrogation regardless of their age. The following section will examine various age groups and some of the difficulties inherent to these groups. Even though typical behavior is being classified and labeled, it is advised to be wary of stereotyping.

Not everyone fits the mold. The assessment phase, or the beginning of an interview or interrogation, is a good time to gauge which respective age group the individual may fit into.

Children

Children are particularly difficult subjects for a number of reasons. Even at relatively young ages, children have had a whole set of experiences that color their ability to understand or tell the truth. In cases regarding children, there are no absolute ages at which certain reactions or abilities occur. It depends on the child's experience and emotional development.

Many times, children are victims of mental or physical abuse, have been threatened, and are just plain scared. These children are very difficult subjects, and it requires an interviewer with the ability to build a rapport with a child. In these situations, an interviewer with special training, such as a psychologist trained in retrieving information from a traumatized child, may be needed.

Who can break the ice with a child, develop a trusting, comfortable relationship and conduct a successful interview? The person who can build a trusting relationship with the child should conduct the interview.

Mistakes made while interviewing children can introduce complicated legal issues involving negligence and malpractice. As previously mentioned, if you are unsure or unaware of the laws regarding interviewing children, seek competent legal counsel.

The Concept of Truth and Right and Wrong

When interviewing a child, you will need to determine the child's understanding of the truth and of right and wrong. Very young children may not have a grasp of the meaning of "truth" or know what a "lie" is. They are at an age at which those terms may have little or no meaning.

When attempting to interview a very young child, it is important to conduct an assessment of the child's understanding of the concepts of truth and right and wrong by asking control questions such as, "Is it wrong to take a cookie without permission?" or "Is it wrong to tell a lie?", prior to the interview. Once the child's understanding is determined and differentiation between right and wrong and truth and lie is made, you can then decide to continue, change approach, or terminate the interview.

Reality vs. Fantasy

You must gain an understanding of what is real in a child's life as opposed to fantasy. In early childhood, many children live in a world composed of reality and fantasy. Within their imagination, they create their own world. Frequently, traumatized children create a fantasy world as a means of protection from the harsh reality of their life. Sometimes, in their minds, fantasy becomes reality. When this occurs, a trained psychologist can be brought in to strip away the fantasy and get to the reality. It is important that while interviewing a child, the interviewer and child reach an agreement of sorts regarding fantasy and reality. By creating some control questions, you can decide if the child is a viable subject. A control question the interviewer might ask is, "Tell me about your mommy." If the child responds by describing her mommy as a fairy princess who can make all the bad things go away, she may be living in a fantasy world. On the other hand, if she responds by describing her mommy as nice and loving, she is probably living in reality.

Observation Skills

Observation skills refer to the ability to competently relay information about an observed event. A child's ability to observe and remember events, then later relate them in an understandable fashion, can create difficulties for the interviewer. Distance, time, and space may have no importance in the life of the child. A long time in a child's life might be five minutes and a giant may be an adult of average height. Again, through conversation with the child, you should be able to gauge the child's perception of distance, time, and space. You can ask control questions such as, "How long did it take you to get here today?" and, "Tell me what happened when you got here?" You should be able to assess the child's understanding of time and ability to recall events based on the responses.

The Interview Setting

Careful attention should be paid to the interview setting when a child is interviewed. Size intimidates children, so it is suggested that you and the child be as close as possible to the same physical level, e.g. eye level. A person towering over a child in a scary place can be positively terrifying. Many facilities have a room with toys and small furniture; this places the child in a setting that is non-threatening. Depending on the situation, you may want to interview the child in her own home on familiar ground.

Leading Questions

Leading questions are questions that inherently imply the desired answer. For example, "It was your mom who picked you up from school, right?" Children are particularly susceptible to leading questions and sometimes will agree with whatever the you say just to get you to go away and leave them alone. An abused child may react positively to almost any question to avoid continued or repeated abuse and will continue to do so as a coping mechanism. When interviewing a child, you need to ask simple, direct questions, but must be careful not to ask leading questions.

The Protective Instinct

The protective instinct refers to a child's instinct to protect their parents. An abused child, even a severely abused one, will often say whatever is necessary to protect the abused party. This usually occurs when there has been a long period of intimidation and threats. It is possible that the child has been returned to the abusing party by the authorities, making the child even more reluctant to cooperate. For the child, it is survival.

Adolescents and Young Adults

The physical and emotional changes that occur during adolescence make it a very difficult time for many people. Fitting in and being one of the groups is at the top of the priority list. Unfortunately, the group selected by the young person may be the worst possible choice. In their eyes, there is nothing worse than a rat, one who sells out his age group or subculture. Suspicious of adults and authority figures, many adolescents and young adults are reluctant to volunteer information. Rapport is everything in dealing with this age group, but unfortunately, not every adult interviewer or interrogator can establish this relationship. If you have trouble in this area, perhaps it's a good idea to defer to someone one knows who has an affinity for dealing with young people.

Peer Pressure and Gang Involvement

Peer pressure and gang involvement are inevitable when working with adolescents. With a strong desire to fit in, young people develop loyalties to their peers, regardless of their group affinity. Often, they are very reluctant to cooperate and will be very protective of their peers. Peer loyalty takes a step to the extreme when the subject or suspect is a gang member. Loyalties are extremely strong, with disloyalty often resulting in the death of the young person. Breaking through a gang member's barrier is very difficult and is met with limited success.

Suspicion of Authority

Adolescents and young adults are intrinsically suspicious of authority. They pass through a naturally rebellious stage when parental, school, or official authority figures are the enemy. Authority figures are viewed as a threat to their lifestyle, people who write them tickets, hassle them continually, and otherwise infringe on their freedom. Sometimes breaking through this tough veneer is quite difficult and requires a unique ability to achieve a rapport with a person within this age group.

History of Abuse

Young persons with long histories of abuse develop a thick protective shell that is hard to penetrate. Patience and compassion are sometimes rewarded with results. Often, a mental health professional is needed to assist in breaking through without causing unnecessary damage in the process.

Adults

Adults are a little less complex and are generally either cooperative or uncooperative, depending on their lifestyle and experiences. A younger interviewer may experience some resistance or resentment when the subject is older and perceives himself as much wiser. A little finesse goes a long way.

Cooperative

Property owners or other adults with a stake in the community are usually quite cooperative. They form the bulk of the victims, witnesses, and complainants.

They generally offer assistance unless they have the misfortune to live in a gang area where their cooperation might be rewarded with retaliation.

Uncooperative

Unfortunately, gang members and "outlaws" grow up into adults, bringing their baggage along with them. Mentally, they are operating much as they did when they were younger. Many times, these individuals have served jail or prison time and make up a subculture that is in and out of custody; they live by their wits and their ability to con others. Having lied most of their lives, they become known as pathological liars. They live a lie and are good at it.

Some adult individuals who otherwise would be quite cooperative have had, from their viewpoint, bad experiences and unfair treatment by law enforcement or other authorities. Again, a little finesse will possibly get some positive results. It takes more patience and effort to gain their trust.

Elderly

Many elderly people suffer in many different ways and degrees from the effects of age. Of primary concern are the afflictions affecting their ability to remember and relate events. Short-term memory loss is one aspect of aging. The elderly may be afflicted with dementia or Alzheimer's disease in various stages of impairment. Too often, the elderly are victimized by criminals and may be unable to give reliable responses to you due to their age-related issues. Careful evaluation is necessary during the early stages of an interview. Compassion and patience are essential virtues of interviewers who work with elderly subjects. However, be wary of stereotyping the elderly.

EMOTIONS

Understanding the mechanics and dynamics of emotions can help you understand the subject's point of view. Emotions occur because the situation has some meaning or consequence to the person. Emotions come into play when the event concerns their goals, interests, motives, and especially their expectations. For example, fear is evident when these matters are threatened, and anger is when the subject feels wronged. Emotions are a reaction to what the subject perceives is happening. This is influenced by past experiences. Emotions change in intensity with the change in intensity of the event and remain for the duration of the event. With time, the emotions will eventually decrease and dissipate. If an emotion is strong enough, it will seem total and overwhelming to the person experiencing it.

Negative Emotions

Negative emotions are the result of negative thoughts. For example,

- Sadness results from thoughts of loss.
- Frustrations result from feelings of unfulfilled expectations.
- Anxiety and panic from thoughts of danger.
- Guilt from a feeling that you are bad.
- Inferiority is a thought or feeling that you are less than others.
- Anger comes from thoughts that you have been treated unfairly.
- Loneliness comes from the thought that you are not loved and are alone.
- Hopelessness comes from thoughts that things will never improve.

If the subject's emotion is addressed, you will increase the chance that the person will want to talk and provide accurate information. First, identify the thought that underlies the emotion or feeling. If you identify the logic and conclusions that the thought is based on, the emotion should dissipate. For example, if someone is feeling angry because of being interviewed, ask why it makes them angry. You would expect a response indicating that the subject feels unfairly treated. You can then address that feeling or perception. You can explain that the interview is merely routine, it is nothing personal and that many people are going to be interviewed, hence it is fair. If someone feels guilty, the emotion is probably based on thoughts that this person is or has been bad. You should tell this person that he is a good person for helping the investigation. This technique is covered in greater detail in the interrogation section of this book.

SUMMARY

A thorough understanding of psychological issues is a critical component of the interview and interrogation process. All interviews are human interactions. To ensure success in this human interaction, the interviewer must have an awareness of the psychological issues affecting the interview. People are all different, yet there are many similarities based on personality, age, perception, and emotion. It is much easier to get the information you want when you understand these similarities and use them to better understand the subject.

DISCUSSION QUESTIONS

- Why is it important to know the different personality classifications and types?
- How might age affect the progress of an interview?
- What perception filters do you find yourself using? Recall a time when your perception filter affected the way you perceived a situation. Was your perception different from those around you?
- Why is it important to identify the source of the subject's emotion?

CHAPTER 4.

THE INTERVIEW

CHAPTER OVERVIEW

The interview is the process of seeking, obtaining, and evaluating information from one with knowledge of events and circumstances. Much of the information acquired in the course of an investigation will be obtained from other people. Therefore, it is important for the investigator to be a skilled interviewer. Getting information is what this chapter is all about. Skilled interviewers plan the interview before it begins, carefully arrange the physical environment, use a variety of question types, and skillfully sequence the questions. An interview transitions into an interrogation when information is revealed that leads the interviewer to view the subject as someone directly involved in the focus of the investigation rather than as a mere source of facts.

OBJECTIVES

To teach the reader how to...

- Plan an interview.
- Identify important factors in preparing the physical environment for the interview.
- Define the types of interview questions.
- Identify six techniques used for sequencing interview questions.
- Define "selective interview".
- Identify when to transition from interview to interrogation.

FIELD INTERVIEWS FOR FIRST RESPONDERS

Frequently, the first person at the scene of an event (e.g. traffic collision, medical aid, or report call) doesn't have very much information about what occurred. People standing at a scene may be witnesses, victims, or even suspects. So the importance of quickly gathering as much information as possible can't be stressed enough. If there was a crime committed, the first person on scene has the best opportunity to solve the crime by conducting a thorough preliminary investigation. Interviewing is the first step in the preliminary investigation process, and those interviews become the backbone of the preliminary investigation.

The following is a simple format that can be used in situations where the events call for an interview setting where the ability to plan is very limited. Later in this chapter, very specific information is provided on conducting a Planned or Follow-up Investigative Interview.

Three-Step Interview Method

The Three Step Interview Method is an easy way to conduct a field interview. It is structured to allow the subject to speak at ease while the interviewer has control over the interview. While you are learning, you must practice simple interviews.

Subject Tells the Story

Listen, keeping the subject on track while giving verbal and non-verbal clues to keep the story flowing. It may not be appropriate to take notes during the first step. During this step, the following is accomplished:

- Establish a rapport with the subject
- Determine what crime, offense, or policy violation, if any, may have occurred
- Determine what law enforcement agency has jurisdiction if this is an issue
- Detect signs of untruthfulness or discrepancies if present
- Determine what action you should take

The Subject Retells the Story, and the Interviewer Takes Notes

Gather identifying information about the subject and ask questions about the incident and guide the subject through the story a second time. During this step, the following is accomplished:

- Determine the chronological order of the event
- Establish any elements of a crime, offense, or policy violation, if present

Read the Notes to the Subject

Read the notes back to the subject. During this step, the following is accomplished:

- The subject can correct errors or may recall additional information
- The interviewer can correct errors or ask additional questions

The use of the Three Step Interview Method adds credibility to the process since the interviewer always uses the same method, following the same three steps, in all interviews. If there is a discrepancy between the subject's courtroom testimony and what's written in the report, the use of the Three Step Method documents how the information was collected and documented.

PLANNED OR FOLLOW-UP INTERVIEW

The scientific method can be used to plan the interview. This is a systematic approach to scientific investigation composed of five steps. It is used by scientists and is one of the best ways of breaking down and analyzing a problem to develop a plan. Use the scientific method during the planning of the interview and investigation. There are five steps:

State the Goal

During this first stage of the scientific method, you must identify the problem. You should define the purpose and path of the interview by breaking down the problem into its constituent parts. Do not make assumptions; stick to facts and observations, making sure any conclusion reached is free of illogical assumptions. This will help identify the desired result of your interview. Identify the reasons for conducting the interview.

Be Objective

You must be sure that prior learning, conditioning, and experiences do not taint, filter, or cloud what you are hearing or concluding. Try to get to the "truth." One of the best phrases is: "Just because you believe something does not mean that it is true." Analyze your own opinions, interpretations, and conclusions by identifying the who, what, when, where, how, and why of each fact, observation, and conclusion.

Gather Information

You should strive to acquire all available information relevant to the topic at hand. This includes gathering facts, observations, opinions, and any other available evidence.

Evaluate

Based on the information gathered thus far, you can begin to draw conclusions. Conclusions should be based on information or evidence. Look for patterns, directions, how conclusions can be drawn, and how these might help reach other conclusions. This is the first stage where you begin to "think" and make what you have work.

Conclude

Make decisions and priorities. At this stage, it is likely that conclusions will be reached and decisions made that will help determine where to go next. This provides the big picture of what has been done previously.

Upon completion of this process, you may have a good idea of what questions need to be asked and in what areas at various stages of the investigation. Of course, this is merely a guide. In any interview, other issues will come up.

With a good plan, you will know how to assess information obtained in an interview and how it may fit into other areas.

PREPARING THE PHYSICAL ENVIRONMENT

The right physical environment is important for an effective interview. This refers to the location where the interview will take place. It should be a safe, neutral location where both you and the person being interviewed will be comfortable.

Personal Space

For the purposes of the interview, you do not want to be too physically close. No two people are alike in their personal space, but generally, the following are the distances most people associate with various comfort zones for interviewing: Touching - up to 20 inches, casual - 1½ to 5 ft., impersonal - 4 to 12 ft., public - 12 ft. +. Casual is probably the best for your interview. If you get too close, the person may become intimidated, defensive or may interpret this as a sexual advance.

A Productive Climate

In general, there are two types of climates that can be created during an interview: Supportive and Defensive.

Supportive Climate

This climate is a nonjudgmental atmosphere in which spontaneous discussion is encouraged. You do not attempt to deceive the subject. You stick to the issues and facts of the case or problem, fostering an atmosphere of mutual trust and respect by demonstrating the ability to understand the subject's feelings, attitudes, and ideas.

Defensive Climate

In this environment, the interviewer may place blame on the subject and may make moral judgments regarding his behavior. The interviewer may manipulate or trick the subject, demonstrating apathy and a condescending attitude.

During the planning stage of the interview, think about the environment where the interview will be conducted. If time and resources permit, perform a mock interview with another colleague to identify unexpected issues that may surface.

Your first impression is a big part of the interview, and therefore your dress and physical appearance are important. Consider whether to dress formally or informally, being cautious about intimidation and officiousness versus relaxation and trust. Your appearance always conveys something to the person being interviewed.

STARTING THE INTERVIEW

By this point, you have already planned the interview using the scientific method. In general, you know where you need to go, what topics to cover, and what facts to obtain. Now, you decide specifically how to proceed with the interview.

To start the interview, the subject should be encouraged to interact freely and accurately. You should greet them enthusiastically using verbal as well as nonverbal signals. Make the subject feel important and that the subject is an integral part of the process. You can do this by letting the subject know that their assistance is important and that others will know of their aid unless the subject wishes to remain anonymous.

Explain to the subject why they were selected for an interview. If appropriate, tell them who else has been interviewed or who recommended that the subject be interviewed. Tell them about the purpose and orientation of the interview, their role in it, and how the information will be used. This tells them that you care about their concerns and involvement.

Next, you should begin to ask the questions. You will notice that the beginning of the interview differs from the beginning of the interrogation. In interrogation, you will spend more time with rapport development and an introductory phase. The interview is part of the information-gathering stage of an investigation; therefore, you may interview many people during the investigation and find only a few who have valuable information. Consequently, building rapport is not as important in an interview. The investigator begins the questioning right away. This section refers to the topics previously addressed, for example, interpersonal skills, communication theory, and emotions.

To maximize the information obtained during an interview and ensure its accuracy, the following is a list of ideas to consider when conducting an interview.

- How does each question affect the person emotionally and psychologically?
- How does each question impact your rapport with your subject?
- Did the subject give the response you were looking for?
- Ask preliminary questions that cover all topics related to the investigation.
- Don't ask leading questions.
- Ask questions that require a concrete answer.
- Think about the subjectivity of a response.
- Specify the depth and scope you want in an answer.

Question Types

There are several types of questions; however, in most cases, there are two categories or ways to ask questions: open-ended and close-ended.

Open-ended questions

These are questions that elicit a narrative response, such as, "Tell me, what happened?" This provides an overall understanding of what the person has to say, their priorities, and their frame of reference. You must listen intently and let the subject know you are listening by responding appropriately. Remember to use both verbal and non-verbal clues, such as nodding head or leaning forward. This will encourage them to dig deeper and give more information than the subject might have otherwise. This type of question helps you see the big picture and learn more from one question than from any other type of question.

Closed-ended questions

These questions are bipolar (yes or no answer), general ("How tall are you?"), or multiple choice ("Was the shirt green, light green, dark green?"). These questions save time and provide more control. The answers are more specific but not as comprehensive as that of open-ended questions. They also make note-taking easier, but they do not encourage a free response. Closed-ended questions are good for reconstructing an event and gathering information from people who are shy. Closed-ended questions also help keep the person's attention. However, it is easier to falsify a response with these types of questions, given that the person will probably understand what response you are looking for. They can pin down an answer that is favorable, although false.

The following types of questions are problematic and should be avoided:

Double-barreled questions

These are questions asked in succession; one question follows another before the subject can answer the first question. This can cause the person to blend the responses or fail to answer one or the other. Also, because this makes you sound in a rush or intent on a conclusion, it can taint the answer.

Examples

Open-ended: "What did you see when you arrived?" "Were there any other people there?" "Did you know anyone there?"

Closed Ended: "What time did you leave your house?" "When did you arrive at the park?" "Who was with you in the car?"

Two questions in one

This type of question creates the same problem as the double-barreled question but is less noticeable to the person being interviewed. It is two questions contained in a single sentence.

Examples

Open-ended: "What did you see when you arrived and did anything look out of place?"

Closed-ended: "Who was there when you arrived and what were their names?"

Leading questions

This is probably the most famous type of question. This is the question that causes the person being asked to feel they are expected to give a certain response. This is a problem because it is likely that you will get what they want to hear, not the truth.

Examples

Open-ended: "You know what happened here, right?" Closed-ended: "It was you who committed the crime, right?"

Emotionally loaded questions

These questions imply that an answer is favorable, making the person being interviewed feel obliged to respond in a favorable way. Though it is like the leading question, it is more sinister in that it would be less obvious to the subject that the question will taint the answer.

Examples

Open-ended: "You wouldn't mind helping those less fortunate, would you?"
Closed-ended: "Would you mind donating your time to help the homeless?"

Sequencing of Questions

The order in which questions are asked is as important as the type of question asked. As one answer can lead to other areas of inquiry, the questions asked first, next, and last can determine whether important areas of information are uncovered. The topics below will help sequence questions.

Funnel questioning

In this technique, you begin with general questions and move to specific questions as the interview progresses. Open-ended questions are generally asked first. This is effective because it does not limit the subject and allows them to communicate opinions and ideas. It is also helpful because it broadens the range of topics and issues addressed. Furthermore, it helps develop rapport and ease any tension that may exist.

Examples

"What did you see when you got there?"
"Who else was there?"
"Did you see anything on the floor next to the chair?"
"Did you see anyone you knew holding a gun?"

Reverse-funnel questioning

This technique is the opposite of funnel questioning. You begin with specific questions, usually close-ended, and move to general questions, usually open-ended. This technique allows the person being interviewed to think about the specifics before being more general. Specific committals can be important to higher generalizations. This also helps the reluctant person start talking. It also has the benefit of getting the memory in gear by asking about specific things, which can then jog the memory about other details.

Examples

"Did you recognize the woman wearing the red coat?" (wait for a response) "Have you met her before?"

"Did you recognize the driver of the car?" (wait for a response and assuming the answer is 'yes') "Tell me more about how you know the driver?"

Alternative sequencing

This pattern of questioning involves using a combination of the funnel and reverse-funnel questioning types in whatever order and amount appears appropriate. If planned properly, it can be a very powerful way of getting as much accurate and thorough information as possible.

Who, What, When, Where, Why, and How

Also known as the big 6, these elements should be covered for each issue and each point discussed in the interview. Frequently, they are asked as follow-up questions.

Examples

- Who – "Who did you see come into the store?"
- What – "What did you hear him say to the clerk?"
- When – "What time did he come into the store?"
- Where – "Where were you standing in the store?
- Why – "Why didn't you call the police right away?"
- How – "How did he get away?"

Transitions

Transitions are words or phrases used to connect two thoughts. Use transitions to flow from one point to the next smoothly and to link each area of questioning. This ensures the logical flow of questions and makes the subject feel that the interview is progressing. One way to transition from one point to the next is to give a summary of what was discussed and link it to the next point.

Example

"You've told me about what you saw the subject do. So now tell me what the clerk did?"

Conclusions

When concluding the interview, give signals that it is ending, provide an overall summary of the information discussed, and express a sense of accomplishment in the interview. As before, explain to the subject what will happen next and how the information the subject provided will be used.

Example

"Thank you very much for your cooperation and all the good information you've provided us. The description of the subject will be very helpful in his apprehension. In a couple of days, someone will call you, if that's okay, and fill you in on what's happened in the case."

OBSERVATION OR INFERENCE RESPONSES

When the subject responds to a question, you should determine whether the response is the result of observation or inference. An observation is something the subject personally witnessed. Observations involve specific incidents that occur during or after the event, but not in the future. An observation most closely matches what actually occurred. An inference is a conclusion drawn from established facts or information. Inferences can be made by anyone and with varying degrees of certainty, e.g. a guess. Any statement about the future or motive is an inference. Be careful to examine whether the information is the result of an inference or an observation. Inferences can be valuable; however, it is important to understand why the person made the inference. Separate what was seen, heard, smelled, or touched from what was inferred.

ACTIVE LISTENING

During the interview, it is imperative that you utilize listening skills. Recall the discussion of communications theory. Communication is the exchange of information between two or more people. It requires two components: the sender/speaker and the receiver/listener. The speaker and the listener must be active participants in the process of communication for it to be effective. A good listener is an active listener and responds to what was said. Active listening includes asking questions that clarify what has been communicated. This helps you determine the subject's frame of reference and builds rapport. Active listening encourages the subject to talk more because they know they are being heard. For example, use encouraging words like, "Yes... continue... I understand". This communicates active listening is in place and connotes a sense of caring. In addition, maintain eye contact, do not allow interruptions, and refrain from doodling or taking notes, which may distract the subject.

Chapter 2 identified six factors that can cause the listening process to break down: distractions, vocabulary, unstated assumptions, schemas, cultural differences, and modes of speech. Be aware of these factors during the interview. It is important to be prepared and to know the facts of the case so you understand how the subject's responses relate to the investigation. If you notice their concentration beginning to wane, you can maintain interest in the interview by linking one thought to the next and integrating what they are hearing into the big picture. Take advantage of the speed of thinking, which is 400 words per minute compared to speech, which averages 120 words per minute. Think about how the subject's responses align with the previously obtained information.

FOLLOW UP QUESTIONS

Most questions require follow-up, as most answers are inadequate. The response may be incomplete, inaccurate, irrelevant, contradictory, or there may be no response at all. These answers can be a result of an unwillingness on the part of the subject, inability due to lack of knowledge or memory, and/or confusion as to what you are asking. Most follow-up questions fall under one of the following six categories:

Clarify the question

The subject may not have understood the question, so you may need to reword or simplify the question.

Repeat the question

If the person evades, re-ask the question or make it less threatening.

Clarify the response

The subject's response may be unclear or incomplete. In this case, ask the subject to elaborate, amplify, and expand the prior answer.

Example

"I don't understand what you mean." "Could you explain what that means?"

Confront the person

This is necessary when the subject's response creates inconsistencies or is an obvious lie.

Example

"What you just said does not appear to be factually correct." "The evidence doesn't support what you said."

Use neutral phrases

Use neutral phrases to encourage the subject to continue talking.

Example

"Yes... I see... continue"

Utilize silence

This allows reflection, communicates more is expected, and shows a willingness to listen.

When asking follow-up questions, keep in mind that interpersonal and psychological issues can arise. For a review of these topics, refer to Chapter 3, Psychological Issues, and the section titled Interpersonal Skills.

MISCELLANEOUS TACTICAL SUGGESTIONS

Hypothetical Scenarios about the Future

Using hypothetical scenarios about future events may stimulate information from the subject. Using the word "if" when discussing the objective or possible outcome of the case may lessen any accusations that may seem implied.

Example

"If the investigation implicates..." is less accusatory than, "When we find..."

Get Important Information First

It is essential for you to collect important information from the subject at the start of the interview. Important information includes the subject's contact information, such as their name, phone number, email, and address. If conditions are adverse, for example, in an emergency, you might only be able to obtain contact information, so the subject can be contacted later when the environment is not so adverse.

Witness Separation

You should separate witnesses as soon as possible. People tend to seek group acceptance and consensus. Witnesses may share stories and adopt the facts and interpretations of other witnesses. While this is not done intentionally, it is human nature, and therefore, witnesses should be separated and interviewed individually as soon as possible. Witness testimony will be discussed in greater detail later in section 2.

Identify the Witness's Emotions

Identify and address a witness's emotions right away. This will help build their confidence and help in the questioning process. Fear is a common emotion in a witness. Use common reassurance to address this emotion. See the Emotions section of Chapter 3 for more information.

Use the Exact Words of The Witness When Appropriate

Sometimes it is necessary to repeat exactly what the subject said to communicate that you heard what was said. This is like reflective listening, except it requires you to use the exact words the subject used. This can also help make a transition into the next question.

Example

"You said you saw the car turn left... Did you notice the speed of the car?"

Recounting what the person said using his exact words can lessen any suspicions that a report is biased. It also prevents you from inferring information, which often occurs when a subject's statement is summarized or paraphrased. It is most appropriate to repeat the subject's exact words when it involves sensitive issues, for example, when it helps establish an element of a crime. When taking notes or for report writing, remember to use quotation marks when noting specific quotes from someone.

Getting Philosophical

Using philosophical phrases is an effective way of transitioning the subject to a new topic or keeping the interview moving. This approach can also be used to take the atmosphere of the interview to another level.

Example

"So, what is really going on here?" or "What does this all mean?"

Use Humor When Appropriate

Using humor in an interview can be helpful because it can take the pressure off and help build rapport. However, it can also be inappropriate. If the person is too deeply immersed in emotion or if the humor is off-color, it can have a destructive effect on the interview. Humor during an interview should be lighthearted and never put other people down. In fact, the interviewer putting himself down in a lighthearted way can be the best humor in an interview.

Self-disclosure

Self-disclosure is when you reveal relevant information about yourself. Self-disclosure is used to build rapport with a subject and normalize their behavior and may include discussing your own feelings and past experiences about the topic or incident.

REMOTE INTERVIEWS

The pandemic has increased the use and prevalence of phone calls and online meetings such as Google Meet, Zoom, Microsoft Teams and similar tools. Remote interviews are more cost effective and convenient. And, some interviewees are more comfortable being in a setting such as at their home, and remotely, as opposed to face-to-face. .

For the Interviewee

- Make sure that there is enough time to devote to the entire interview.
- Consider the time of day: will they get hungry or tired?
- Be sure they know how to use the technology such as how to join, how to set audio and video settings.
- Understand distractions that may exist on their end like, children, spouses, animals, co-workers, background noise, possible deliveries (e.g. Amazon), looking out a window etc. You should ask the person to remove distractions if possible.

- As the interviewer, you should be aware of any other persons in the interviewees room and whether you are being recorded. In some jurisdictions, it is a crime to eavesdrop on, or record, a conversation without the express consent of all participants.
- Have the interviewee close out other applications they may be running to avoid distraction and to ensure technical issues do not arise.
- Inform the interviewee that they should be certain that no one else in their location should be able to listen to, or watch, the interview unless they are a necessary party to the interview. This helps maintain privacy and confidentiality. The presence of others on their side may dissuade the interviewee from disclosing information. You may need to ask them if there is anyone else in the room with them.

For the Interviewer

- Everything that applies to the interviewee also applies to you.
- Your background may include books, degrees/diplomas and certifications. This helps establish credibility. However, anything that suggests authority or punishment, may reduce rapport.
- Assist the interviewee with any technical issues such as learning how to use an online meeting tool (e.g. Zoom).
- If you are going to record the interview, make sure you get the consent of all participants and, if there are others in the room with you, make sure others know that they are present and can hear what is being said.

THE SELECTIVE INTERVIEW

Before getting into the meat of this topic, the investigators should understand that certain "workplace" investigations are very technical and are often fraught with very involved legal issues specifically directed at what the investigator can and cannot do or what they can or cannot ask. Re-review the Legal Concerns / Workplace Investigations coverage earlier if needed. It is highly recommended that these issues be thoroughly researched by a legal professional well-versed in this topic.

The selective interview is a hybrid of an interview and an interrogation. The selective interview is used to narrow down many people to a select few. The selective interview may turn into an interrogation or it may help identify other subjects to interrogate later. The selective interview might turn up little or nothing; however, it will allow you to weed out those people who may have a little probability of involvement.

During the selective interview process, you need to include everyone who could possibly be involved in the incident. This demonstrates that everyone is being treated fairly and equally. It also enables you to "net in" as much information as possible.

If time and money permit, you should conduct appropriate and relevant background information on each person to be interviewed as well as prepare a list of common questions to be asked of everyone during each interview. A thorough understanding of all relevant evidence and information should be conducted.

When conducting selective interviews, you need to first prioritize the interviews. Generally, managers are interviewed first because they tend to have the most information about the situation and to decide who to interview next.

Next, you should question all people least likely to be involved in the focus of the investigation. By doing this, you collect as much information as possible before confronting anyone. If an involved subject is unknown, or if there are multiple possible subjects involved, you may not be able to make this decision. The same is true if, during the interviews of those believed not to be involved, you develop information that links others to the target(s) of the investigation.

As a rule of thumb, interviewers/investigators should not ask subjects questions that they don't already know the answer to. This is why involved subjects are interviewed last in most cases. Remember that interviews with involved subjects require the most time and energy, so plan accordingly.

At the beginning of each interview, you establish their credibility and explain why the interviews are being conducted. Use a professional greeting and/or introduction. Interviews are non-accusatory.

As usual, the questions you may ask will flow from the evidence and relevant plausible theories. However, selective interviews utilize other types of questions that can be very effective.

Possible selective interview questions

Following is a list of statements and questions that may be used in a selective interview:

- "Do you know who is or is not involved in the incident?"

This determines if the subject knows of anyone involved in the incident. This is very useful to help to scope the investigation.

- "Did you do it?"

This determines if the subject is involved by asking directly. How you do this will be addressed later.

- "Who had the opportunity to commit the act?" "What would be the easiest way to do it?"

These questions help to determine who the subject thinks would have the best opportunity to commit the act or the easiest way to do it. Again, this is one of the best ways to rope in as much information as possible.

- "How do you feel about the investigation?"

This helps establish how the subject feels about the investigation and how the subject is being treated or investigated.

- "What should happen to the person who did it?"

This helps with understanding what the subject thinks would be an appropriate punishment for those suspected of underlying targets (e.g. wrongdoing) of the investigation. An involved subject might offer a lighter sentence or suggest a second chance for those involved.

- "Is it ever okay to do it?"

This helps understand if the subject thinks there are times when it is okay to commit acts in question.

- "Why do you think someone would do this?"

This type of question determines why the subject believes someone would commit certain acts relevant to the investigation. If the person is an involved person, this answer may be the actual reason why they did it.

The purpose of asking these questions is to obtain information that helps determine how each subject thinks and feels about the investigations, to determine their involvement or lack of involvement, and if the subject is involved, how.

In conclusion, be sure you have the subject's contact information, conclude the interview and explain where the investigation may go next.

TRANSITION TO INTERROGATION

As an interview progresses and questions produce answers that lead you to believe the subject is an involved, it's time to mentally shift gears and carefully move into interrogation mode.

A note about the definition of "interrogation"

The term interrogation often brings up notions of heat lamps, yelling, finger pointing and an overbearing attitude. Modernly, these approaches have fallen to the wayside for ethical and legal reasons. And, frankly, they are often detrimental to the getting to the truth. So, when we use the term "interrogation," we mean that our line of questioning considers facts that flesh out the legal, regulatory or policy factors in the investigation.

Legal issues

This transition poses a host of legal questions the investigator must know the answer to or have advice or legal counsel readily available.

At this point in the interview where you are considering transition to interrogation, you have some options available. You can continue, take a break and confer with associates and begin the process again as an interrogation, or postpone the interrogation pending additional information.

There are additional factors to consider when deciding to change from an interview to an interrogation. Is the environment right for the interrogation? Is there enough time available? Is the location appropriate? How confident are you that an admission or a confession can be obtained? How complete and thorough is the investigation? If the factors justifying an immediate interrogation are not present, it may be better to save the time of an interrogation for later.

As the transition occurs, control shifts to the interrogator, who will begin to offer rationalizations and other approaches to lessen the involved subject's (or, as we will refer to them in the next chapters, the 'suspect') resistance to make an admission or a confession. The subject may not make any truthful statements unless it serves their purpose to do so. Whatever the decision, this is a crucial part of the process and will require all your skills and experience.

SUMMARY

A considerable amount of the information obtained through the course of an investigation comes from interviews. Interview skills are the most important tool in an investigator's toolbox. In order to maximize the effectiveness of the interview, the investigator should plan the interview, prepare for the physical environment, and be familiar with various interview questions and techniques.

DISCUSSION QUESTIONS

- What are the steps in the Three Step Interview?
- What are the five steps of the scientific method?
- What is the advantage of asking open-ended interview questions?
- What is the advantage of asking close-ended interview questions?
- Explain the difference between observation responses and inference responses.
- List three examples of follow-up questions.

CHAPTER 5.

PREPARING FOR THE INTERROGATION

CHAPTER OVERVIEW

Before getting into our coverage of this topic, it cannot be stressed enough that this interrogation is a skill that is best attained by formal training and experience. It is more responsible to suggest that proper interrogation skills and knowledge should come from online and in-person training programs created for this purpose rather than from a single text. This author has attended (and obtained certification from) one such in-person training program and it was found to be invaluable and, frankly, entirely necessary for the development of interrogation skills. As well, performing interrogations with a properly-trained, seasoned interrogator by this author was performed to further hone skills.

Below are some possible training resources that you may choose to attend. Each offers techniques and methods that have some similarities but they do differ in significant ways. If you are employed by an agency or enterprise, there may be guidelines and requirements in place which should be researched. The resources are the following though this is not an exhaustive list:

- The PEACE method (https://en.wikipedia.org/wiki/PEACE_method_of_interrogation#)
- Wicklander-Zulawski (https://www.w-z.com)
- The Reid Technique (https://en.wikipedia.org/wiki/Reid_technique)
- The Kinesic Interview (Walters, Stan B. Principles of Kinesic Interview and Interrogation, Second Edition. (CRC Press, 2003)).

There is one publication that has been referenced by many as a great general guide to how to approach interrogation from a philosophical perspective as well as a technical resource (Principles on Effective Interviewing for Investigations and Information Gathering, May 2021, retrieved from https://interviewing-principles.com). We are quoting from one page of this publication (reprinted with permission):

"Information-Gathering Techniques

113. Active listening helps the interviewer process the information provided by the interviewee. By listening actively, the interviewer shows that they are following what the interviewee is saying and making efforts to understand. The interviewer takes care not to lead an interviewee inadvertently by using verbal or visual cues, including sounds, gestures or questions, which may be interpreted as agreeing or disagreeing with what the person is saying.

114. The interviewee should be invited to explain in their own words their involvement in, or knowledge or recollection of the matter under scrutiny, and should be allowed to respond fully. This can then be probed for further detail to fill any gaps or explain discrepancies.

115. The interviewer should not generally interrupt the interviewee or break their train of thought and always remain attentive to information provided by the interviewee in order to notice important details and identify specific topics requiring follow-up. Not interrupting is supplemented by making use of silence where appropriate. By remaining quiet, the interviewer signals that it is acceptable to take time to stop and think, and that the interviewer is willing to wait in order to get more details.

116. The type of questioning employed in an interview contributes to achieving the desired objectives and overall outcomes. The aim is to obtain as much voluntary and uncontaminated information as possible. Each question should have a purpose and be asked in a non-judgemental way. The language used should be clear and avoid technical terms or jargon and acronyms.

117. Open-ended questions, such as 'explain to me,' 'tell me' or 'please describe,' reduce the risk of contaminating the interviewee's memory; they are more likely to produce more details and fuller answers, which are less likely to have been influenced by the interviewer.

118. Probing questions, such as 'who,' 'what' and 'where', may be necessary to obtain more detail once a response has been given to an open-ended question. They help in obtaining additional relevant information and identifying specific gaps and inconsistencies that require further exploration. Interviewees may also reveal something that they have not previously disclosed.

119. The strategic use of information can help guide the interview to ensure the information being elicited is relevant to the purpose of the interview.

120. Accurate summaries of what the interviewee has said may facilitate the positive progression of the interview and assist the interviewer and interviewee in recalling important details. However, poorly worded summaries may contaminate the interviewee's account and introduce bias or inaccuracies. Interviewees may also interpret inaccurate summarising as an indication that the interviewer was not listening or is trying to manipulate their account.

Encountering Reluctance

121. Interviewers may encounter interviewees who are reluctant to talk and therefore should anticipate how they will handle such situations. Not wanting or agreeing to answer questions may be a deliberate choice. For example, suspects in criminal cases have the right to remain silent and some will exercise this right. This decision must always be respected and has no bearing on the interviewee's right to the presumption of innocence.

122. Reasons why an interviewee might be reluctant to talk can include general anxiety or uncertainty about the process, especially if the person has never been involved in such a situation before. Fear can also play a part; for example, a fear of police and other state officials, or fear of adverse repercussions to themselves or others if it becomes known that they have talked to the authorities. Interviewees may also be psychologically affected by what they have seen, heard or been through. Reluctance to talk may also be due to the interviewee's personal reactions to the interviewer or interpreter.

123. It is also possible that an interviewee may be willing to provide information but is unable to do so. This can be because they did not have the relevant information to begin with, or they failed to register the details. It may be that the passage of time or things that interviewees have experienced have led them to forget the original details or made them unable to retrieve them from their memory.

124. Interviewers will increase the likelihood of conducting an effective interview by expressing a respectful awareness of why someone may be reluctant to talk, clarifying that any information provided will be kept confidential within the limits allowed by law, and respecting any continuing refusal to talk. Interviewers should not draw negative inferences from the interviewee's failure or refusal to answer questions and should remain non-judgemental when an interviewee may make admissions to crimes or convey embarrassing information."

What follows in the remainder of the interrogation section is content that that we offer that is a culmination of formal training and experience that this author has developed over decades of experience performing thousands of interviews and interrogations ranging from simple to very complex matters. It provides possible approaches, techniques and ideas to give you, the interrogator, an understanding of what interrogation is, and how it transitions and flows. What you choose to utilize is a professional journey that should be developed with understanding of appropriate and relevant laws, department policy and adherence to accepted standards and common sense.

During the course of the interview, information may be uncovered that leads the interviewer to view the suspect as a target of the investigation. When this happens, the interview gradually shifts to an interrogation. An interrogation is the questioning of an individual suspected of some liability or culpability. During the interrogation, the suspect is interviewed and asked about his involvement in the target of the investigation, e.g. crime, tort, policy violation. Preparing for the interrogation involves gathering information about the suspect and the event, selecting an appropriate interrogator, preparing the physical environment, and considering issues that may affect the interrogator-suspect relationship.

OBJECTIVES

To teach the reader how to...

- Outline the background information that should be obtained before an interrogation.
- Identify the attributes of a good interrogator with regard to a specific case.
- Determine the physical environment of the interrogation.
- Identify issues that may affect the interrogator-suspect relationship.

THE PURPOSE OF THE INTERROGATION

It should be noted that the term "suspect" is used during the coverage of this part of the investigation rather than the subject. This merely helps to distinguish that information sought from the person being interviewed includes more about that person's direct involvement and possible culpability. As well, the term interrogator rather than interviewer will be used for the same reason. It is not intended to imply guilt or culpability by using these terms. These terms are commonplace in this area of professional practice. As discussed earlier, the information-gathering process, and the interviews/interrogations, should be performed appropriately and with an eye towards getting to the truth, whatever the outcome (e.g. whether the truth establishes inculpatory or exculpatory information or something in between).

The difference between an interrogation and an interview is that the goal of the interrogation is to establish a suspect's involvement and explore other possible areas of culpability while the goal of the interview is to gather general information.

The suspect should be interrogated from a broad base of inquiry in order to collect as much information as possible. Using this technique allows the investigator to elicit information without directly asking for it. Prior to the interrogation, the investigator identifies a goal. They consider the underlying reasons for the investigation in determining the goal. However, the goal should always be stated with an eye towards an even assumption that the suspect may not be involved as you might expect. Do not become myopic because of a poorly stated goal.

BACKGROUND INFORMATION

Gathering background information relevant to the investigation is a fundamental part of preparing for the interrogation. The more you know before the interrogation, the better you will be able to evaluate the information obtained during the interrogation. Relevant background information includes witness interviews, factual background, investigative reports, online research, and any other legally available tool.

The Suspect

Part of the background investigation includes learning about the suspect. It is important to know how a suspect has reacted in previous interviews and interrogations. Discuss his behavior with those who have previously interrogated him. Has the suspect been cooperative, truthful, or belligerent? Any information regarding previous behavior could be invaluable if known prior to the interrogation.

It is also prudent to consider a suspect's desire to cooperate. The suspect may not want to be considered a "narc" or a "snitch" or may not want to get a close friend or family member in trouble. Perhaps the suspect doesn't want to get involved. Perhaps the suspect does not like the police or investigators. All of these factors affect their willingness to cooperate.

It is a good idea to keep in mind the suspect's personality type. Recall the personality types discussed in Chapter 3: Psychological Issues. You should have some understanding of the suspect's basic personality type before the interrogation. You can further develop an understanding of the suspect's personality by conducting a baseline assessment, which is discussed in detail in Chapter 6: The Interrogation.

Other suspects

When preparing for the interrogation, you may want to consider the suspect in relation to other suspects. One suspect might have useful information about another suspect. In this case, you might allude to the idea that the other suspect(s) have been saying incriminating things about them. If there is more than one suspect to interrogate, you must decide who to interrogate first. Often, you will begin with the person most likely to confess or with the suspect who may have the most information. The reason for using this approach is that you will obtain specific information from these suspects that can be used against the other suspects. Useful information includes details about the events such as the people involved, what was done, and how it was done. You can then use this information to increase their credibility with other suspects or identify lies.

The Interrogator

Careful consideration must be taken when selecting the interrogator. The person conducting the investigation may decide to conduct the interrogation or they may select another interrogator who is better suited for the particular situation. There are several factors to be considered when making this decision. They include:

- Is there someone who has successfully interrogated the suspect before?
- Is there already a rapport developed with an interrogator?
- Are there negative feelings between the potential interrogator and the suspect?
- Did the potential interrogator fail to get a confession in past interrogations with the suspect?
- Has the suspect been prosecuted by the potential interrogator before?

Often the person who has conducted the investigation up to the point of the interrogation is the best person to conduct the interrogation as they know the most about the investigation and therefore will know what statements may not be truthful.

The interrogator should not be someone that the suspect sees as beneath them. For example, some people of status view police officers as "public servants" and private investigators as security guards. If this is the case, it might be wise to have a supervisor or "high-ranking" individual conduct the interrogation.

The most effective interrogator is one who is likable, emotionally mature, and comfortable in many types of situations. They should be polite but firm. Generally, the person should have the following traits or qualities:

- Be observant and have a quick perception.
- Employ many techniques, not just a few favorites.
- React well under stress.
- Have an outward sense of self-esteem and self-confidence.
- Have a basic understanding of psychological factors regarding how people think, feel, and react.
- Use common sense and have a thorough understanding of the incident being investigated.
- Have knowledge of relevant legal issues, especially as it concerns interviews and interrogations.

An interrogator who does not possess these traits may not feel comfortable in the role of an interrogator and, for this reason, may become anxious or frustrated, hindering the interrogation.

THE PHYSICAL ENVIRONMENT

When choosing the location for an interrogation, the first and foremost consideration is investigator safety. All sharp objects or anything that could be used as a weapon should be kept out of the reach of the suspect and preferably out of the room.

During the interrogation, you want to create a non-threatening environment in which the suspect's attention is focused on the resolution of the problem rather than the potential punishment or consequence. The ideal room is small, private, and free from distractions. It should be approximately 10 x 12 feet in size and contain a small desk and two comfortable chairs. Generally, the chairs are arranged facing each other with nothing between them. This setup is used so you can see the suspect's body to watch for nonverbal behavior. Consider issues related to the suspect not feeling free to leave, such as blocking the doorway or cornering them in one part of the room or another.

Privacy is critical during interrogation because it is likely the suspect will confide very personal information, such as an admission of a crime or the implication of another suspect. Their reputation, job, or personal freedom may be on the line. The suspect will not feel safe confiding in this information if the suspect thinks others can hear what they are saying.

Interruptions can also hinder the interrogation. They break the momentum or mood of an interrogation; therefore, it is critical that participants turn off cell phones and radios, and that the interrogator requests from others that there be no outside interruptions.

Other distractions that can interfere with the interrogation should be removed and include pictures in the room, office supplies, and items that draw attention to the authority, such as handcuffs, police radios, and penal codes. Removing these distractions allows the interrogator to gauge the suspect's nervous behavior. For example, if the suspect has things the suspect can fiddle with, this takes the edge off of his nervous energy, thus lessening the interrogator's ability to see what questions and issues may cause them discomfort. Outward signs of discomfort are significant because they may be signs of guilt or untruthfulness. Also, if the suspect has something distracting to look at, it will cause a break in eye contact, which disrupts your ability to read behavior. Reading behavior is a tool you can use, which will be covered in detail in Chapter 6: The Interrogation.

Props

"Props" such as a thick case file, and digital media that may contain electronic evidence (such as video), may be used in the interrogation room to help establish the credibility of the investigation and how it may have implicated the suspect. These props may or may not contain actual evidence. In the early stages of the interrogation, you do not want to draw too much attention to props. This might cause the suspect to become overly curious about them and begin asking what they are and what significance they have. He may then ask you to start proving the case, which is not appropriate at this point in the interrogation. Many discourage this type of activity on ethical (and perhaps legal) grounds, so use your best judgment and consult appropriate advice as needed. In some states, it is not legal to lie to a suspect about the evidence you have.

Evidence in the Interrogation Room

Actual evidence can be used in the interrogation to help bolster and enhance the interrogation. During the interrogation, you may ask the suspect to view documents and other evidence, and acknowledge what the evidence is and how it was used in the incident. Bringing evidence into the interrogation may also elicit information that fills gaps in the investigation. Any evidence introduced in the interrogation should be safeguarded to prevent contamination or destruction.

Recording the Interrogation

On occasion, you may decide to audio or videotape the interrogation. There are several special considerations to be taken when using recording devices. Prior to the interrogation, the equipment should be checked to ensure it is in good operating condition and background noise in the interrogation room is eliminated. At the beginning of the recording, the investigator records the day, time, and who is present.

Before the discussion begins, you record the participants' consent to be recorded and ask them to speak one at a time during the interrogation. It is essential for you to know the law regarding recording interrogations, especially if it is secretly taped. Recording someone without their consent is a crime in many states. When using an audiotape, if the suspect nods "yes" or makes another gesture, you ask them to provide a verbal response, so it can be recorded. If something sounds garbled, the person is asked to repeat it clearly.

Smoking

The question of whether or not smoking should be allowed in an interrogation is common. Usually, it is not a good idea. Smoking is an outlet for nervous habits and may give the suspect comfort. If the suspect is comfortable, the suspect will not be stressed, and stress is what creates most of the nonverbal behavioral cues that may be indicative of dishonesty. However, if it appears appropriate, you may allow it and note it in the report as an indication of how the suspect was treated fairly.

ISSUES AFFECTING THE INTERROGATOR - SUSPECT RELATIONSHIP

In order for an interrogation to be successful, you must establish a relationship with the suspect. Two factors that affect the interrogator-suspect relationship are rapport and a sense of control.

Rapport

Rapport is a relationship of mutual trust. It is one of the most important factors in creating a successful interrogation. You have a good rapport with the suspect when the suspect trusts you and views you as a person rather than an authority figure. As this sense of mutual respect and trust develops, the suspect is more likely to disclose critical information.

You develop a rapport with a suspect through your verbal and nonverbal behavior during the interrogation. Rapport begins to develop at the first contact. You lay the foundation for rapport by greeting the suspect with an introduction, smile, and handshake. You then proceed to get to know the suspect by engaging in personal conversation rather than jumping right into the interrogation. At this time, you ask the suspect questions about them, their interests, and hobbies. You connect with the suspect by identifying similar interests while practicing the listening skills discussed in Chapter 2.

Supportive and non-officious behavior develops rapport. Your speech is also important when building rapport. Speech patterns, tone, speed of delivery, and pitch all come together to present a particular demeanor. You can use this to your advantage to help the suspect feel more secure, trusting, and open.

Empathy

You can also use specific techniques to build rapport. One of those techniques is empathy, e.g. "putting yourself in someone else's shoes." When you use empathy, you take the suspect's point of view and imagine what it must be like to be that person. You then communicate your thoughts and feelings verbally to the suspect. You want the suspect to understand that you know what the suspect is going through. It takes great skill and finesse to effectively use empathy. If this is not done correctly, it can sound condescending or patronizing.

Synchrony

Another technique used to develop rapport is called synchrony. Synchrony is when you mirrors the suspect's tone of voice, gestures, posture, and overall style of communicating. For example, if the suspect speaks slowly, you slow down your speech.

The synchrony should not be obvious to the suspect. You do not want it to appear that you are mocking or ridiculing the suspect. You must take care when using this technique. You should not engage in street language or try to sound like part of the "gang" unless you have a similar background; this might result in your seeming insincere.

Despite the urge or justification, you should avoid using profanity. This will only hurt your credibility.

Engaging in synchrony with the suspect may make them feel like you on the same "wavelength", at least emotionally. Like empathy, synchrony requires considerable skill and finesse.

Building rapport is not always easy. It may take a great deal of effort and self-control in the event of a particularly heinous crime. Often it requires you to put aside your personal views and beliefs and accept a value system that conflicts with your own. However, you are a professional and not on a personal vendetta. You can communicate this to the suspect through your words and actions.

You can tell a good rapport has been established when the suspect appears relaxed. The suspect leans forward during communication, maintains eye contact, and uses first names when appropriate. A poor rapport will be just the opposite. The suspect will refer to you as sir, madam, or officer. They will sit back and appear withdrawn and avoid eye contact. The suspect may clasp their hands in front of their face, or mouth, or they may cross their legs, clench their fists or stand up as if to leave.

Control of the Interrogation

It is your role to maintain control of the interrogation. The suspect may think they have control and react adversely when they sense they are losing control. They may get angry or begin acting superior. Suspects begin engaging in undesirable behavior to gain control. This includes insults, lies, and profanity. You must not be affected by this behavior because this gives the suspect the belief that the suspect has power and control. You must maintain your control by communicating your expectations for behavior. You communicate these expectations with verbal and nonverbal signals. For example, if the suspect begins insulting you, you can put your hand up as an indication to the suspect to stop talking as you redirect the conversation to the relevant topic.

Often, a suspect will respond to your expectations without even knowing it. This is because people like to conform and to be accepted by others. If you create the expectation of getting the truth and all of it, this expectation will be communicated. If you maintains a sense of neutrality and attempt to understand why the suspect is exhibiting negative behavior, it will leave the door open for cooperation in the future. This does not mean that you accept or condone the suspect's behavior, you are just trying to understand it.

Above all, you must not get caught up in the "I will get you" attitude. When this happens, you are no longer the negotiator, and instead you become the reason that you did not get the information needed from the suspect. However, if you do get pulled off guard, it is best to apologize quickly, and then get back on track.

You may want to conduct a mock interview/interrogation to practice maintaining authority in appropriate ways.

OTHER FACTORS TO CONSIDER

Conducting a thorough and effective interrogation is not a simple task and takes great skill and practice. The following factors are offered to help you improve those skills and get as much advantage as possible during the interrogation process.

Questions

You usually have specific questions you want to cover in the interrogation; however, it is not a good idea to have only a scripted set of questions. The interrogation should be free and conversational. A good interrogator tries to get as much information from the suspect as soon as possible before the suspect realizes they are a target of the investigation. This allows you to get unfiltered information offered freely. The suspect may not realize what he is saying and may offer information that could be used later. For example, the suspect's alibi or other explanations can be expanded and reconfirmed. This might later be used to discredit the suspect if he has lied or changes his story.

Note Taking

During the beginning stages of the interrogation, when you are trying to build rapport, it is not recommended that you take notes. It can be distracting and interfere with rapport development. You may take notes later during the summarization of the interrogation with the suspect.

Sharing Information with the Suspect

It is usually not a good idea for you to tell the suspect what you know. This may be a breach of confidence with other suspects, it may result in the defamation of another, or it may tell the suspect exactly how to build his alibi and how to explain away his involvement.

A subtler reason is to test the suspect's honesty. If the suspect tells you something you already know to be true, it is a good indication that the suspect is being somewhat honest. You may tell a suspect that you have a lot of information and, therefore, you will know if he is being truthful.

Types of Suspects

There are countless types of suspects you will encounter in the course of your career. The following is a brief description of four qualities that a suspect might exhibit that you likely to encounter.

Volunteering Information

If a suspect volunteers information, it may indicate that he is being truthful. Truthful people tend to be spontaneous and natural. He wants to help the investigation and dig deep for information without appearing overly friendly or helpful. His movements vary in intensity and frequency.

On the other hand, untruthful suspects are not spontaneous and do not volunteer additional information. His philosophy is that the less that is said, the less often he must lie and the less that can be later verified as untrue. Furthermore, untruthful suspects do not show a variation in intensity in gestures, which are rigid, repetitive, and contrived.

Innocent Liar

An innocent liar refers to a person who lies unintentionally. This type of person is eager to please and will tell you what he thinks you want to hear. You can identify this type of person because they will appear too anxious to please.

Good Liars

Good liars are suspects who lie out of arrogance and overconfidence. He prides himself on his ability to trick, as such he may not be as stressed as others and will respond differently, generally more adversarial, when challenged.

Complainer

The complainer refers to a suspect who habitually complains. In this situation, you can use active listening to facilitate communication about the suspect's complaints. Once the complaints have been heard and validated, you will need to decide if they warrant further action. Whatever you decide, you need to communicate your decision to the suspect. Usually, if the complainer feels attended to, his attitude will change.

Interrogator's Personal Preparation

Your final steps in preparing for the interview include your own personal preparation. Remember to eat something so the stomach doesn't growl, use the bathroom to maintain personal comfort, make any important phone calls to avoid distractions, and try a psychological pick-me-up. Engaging in a few stretching exercises, deep breaths, or brisk walks are effective ways of loosening tension and redirecting emotions into positive energy.

SUMMARY

An interrogation occurs when the subject of the interview becomes a suspect in the investigation. When preparing for the interrogation, you should gather background information on the suspect and the events, carefully select an appropriate interrogator, prepare the physical environment, and consider issues that may affect the interrogator-suspect relationship.

DISCUSSION QUESTIONS

- What is the difference between an interrogation and an interview?
- What would you do to build rapport with a suspect during an interrogation?
- What is the most important factor to be considered when creating the physical environment for the interview?

CHAPTER 6.

THE INTERROGATION PROCESS

CHAPTER OVERVIEW

During the interrogation, the investigator confronts the suspect regarding their involvement in the crime or incident. Basic interrogation strategies include knowing the suspect, controlling the interrogation through nonverbal communication, and using various types of questions. In addition, you should be familiar with techniques used to elicit cooperation from the suspect during the interrogation if necessary. During the course of the interrogation, the suspect is likely to engage in deception and denial before making an admission or confession. Following a suspect's admission or confession, you take a written statement from the suspect.

OBJECTIVES

To teach the reader how to...

- Define specific interrogation techniques.
- Identify the types of questions to be asked during an interrogation.
- Identify verbal and nonverbal signs of deception, denial, and acceptance.
- Identify types of accusations.
- Define rationalization with regard to an interrogation.
- Distinguish between admission and confession.
- Define and understand the written statement.

STARTING THE INTERROGATION

At the start of the interrogation, you have assembled background information on the suspect and the case and have considered many of the issues that have been addressed in this book. The location of the interrogation has been selected, and a suspect is present. At the outset, you should sell the idea of the interview to the suspect. You do this by discussing a need you have with the suspect and how the interrogation will fulfill this need. Perhaps there is a need to resolve a case or to give a family closure of the crime or event. This approach is used to get the suspect to "buy in" to the interrogation. The word "interrogation" should not be used when discussing the interrogation with the suspect; interview would be a more appropriate word.

Nonverbal Impact

Mannerisms can affect how a suspect will respond. You want to be as constructive as possible. Are your postures rigid or lazy? Are your gestures short and quick? Are your legs crossed, arms folded, showing disinterest, or lack of respect? Your behavior may be sending messages to the suspect that you are not professional, that you may have an alternative agenda, or are not sincere. This damages rapport and the quality and quantity of information you will get from the suspect.

The interrogation usually begins with you reviewing the suspect's personal information, including their full name, age, address, and telephone number. Next, you begin the questioning with an open-ended question, for example, "Tell me what happened on the evening of September 12." This gives the suspect the opportunity to give a free and open narrative account of the incident. As you give a narrative, you use transitional phrases such as "I see... I understand... uh huh" to express interest and keep the narrative moving. If the suspect veers from the subject, you remind them of the last relevant thing that was said and then allow them to carry on. During the narrative, you are cognizant of the suspect's biases and other perceptual issues that may cause the information he is giving to become colored.

Following the narrative, you move into the closed-ended questions to narrow the information down and further explore. At this point, the suspect should be ready to discuss discrepancies if necessary.

The Length of the Interrogation

There is no set length for an interrogation, however, it should be a reasonable length of time. Usually, this is one to two hours. If it begins to go longer, you should begin to examine why. Perhaps you have the wrong suspect or have not been able to develop sufficient rapport with the suspect. The circumstances of the interrogation, such as the type of crime or event, the special needs of the suspect, or the atmosphere, will also affect its length. There is significant case law regarding interview and interrogation methods and duration, so it is recommended that you review the law and consult with your supervisor or legal counsel if necessary.

USE THE RIGHT APPROACH

The initial introductory phase may be informal, friendly, and simple. Ultimately, the interrogation may move to a less friendly territory. From here on in, this book will discuss approaches and techniques that may deviate from the tone of the initial phases of the interrogation. It begins here with some thoughts that approach the new direction the interrogation might take.

There are several approaches that can be used during an interrogation. Using the right approach can make or break the interrogation. You choose what approach to use based on the specifics of the case and the type of suspect. This book will briefly cover eight approaches in the next few pages that an interrogator might use. It will be covered more later and in greater depth.

Tough Love Approach

This philosophy suggests negative consequences for undesirable behavior with the rationale that you are pointing out the consequence in the interests of the suspect. An example of the tough love approach might be to say, "I'm only trying to make your situation the best it can be."

Handling Lies

Handling lies refers to how you respond when you know the suspect is lying. You may let the suspect carry on and commit to the lie, digging himself into a hole. Once the suspect is committed to the lie, you confront the lie directly. It is especially effective when you take a soft approach such as, "Could you be mistaken? Is it possible you are in error? Could we go over this again because your memory doesn't reflect the facts?"

Cooperation with the Suspect

You may use incentives to enlist the suspect's cooperation. In most cases, you cannot make any promises about leniency, but you can let the suspect know that you will inform others that the suspect was cooperative and truthful. This is an effective means of motivating the suspect to tell the truth. You might say, "If you cooperate and tell me who else was involved, I will let the District Attorney know about your cooperation."

Hidden Agenda

You have a hidden agenda when you place important information in an unimportant part of the question. For example, to find out how a burglary suspect entered a house, you might ask, "When you entered the house, did you have a weapon? And by the way, you came through the window, door...?" In this question, the emphasis is placed on a weapon, therefore the suspect will be guarded when answering that part of the question. In the mind of the suspect, the secondary question is trivial in relation to the first question. Therefore, he will be more likely to answer it honestly.

Minimize the Offense

In this approach, you take the suspect's point of view and offer rationalizations for the act. You may say, "We've all done something wrong at some point in our lives," or "Theft isn't the worst thing anyone has ever done." This approach is effective for several reasons. First, it removes the perception of authority from you and makes the suspect view you as a human. Second, it minimizes the offense, thereby reducing the guilt the suspect feels.

Identify With the Suspect

Identifying with the suspect is like minimizing the offense. This is when you use self-disclosure to identify with the suspect. More importantly, the suspect will have the perception that he can identify with you. When using this strategy, you might say, "I have done this before," or "I had a brother who was busted for..." The suspect will feel that you can relate to him increasing rapport and communication. However, this technique can sound patronizing or insincere if used inappropriately.

Catharsis

Ask the suspect how he feels about the events or the investigation. This helps to relieve stress and increases a bond (for rapport). In the Susan Smith case (November 1994) murder suspect, Susan Smith reported her children missing and nine days later confessed to killing them. During one interrogation, Sheriff Wells told Susan that he had the proof that she'd killed her children. She asked him to pray with her and they did, and at the close, the Sheriff said, "Lord, we know that all things will be revealed to us in time." He looked at Susan and said, "Susan, it is the time." She responded by saying, "I am so ashamed. I am ashamed. You don't understand, my children are not all right." She went on to confess to killing them.

Posing A Hypothetical

Posing a hypothetical situation is an effective means of finding out why the suspect is lying or unwilling to talk about something. You create a hypothetical situation and ask the suspect their opinion. For example, "If John Doe had taken the money, what reason do you think he would have for doing it?" or "If John were asked if he had done it and then was not truthful about it, what reason would he have for being untruthful?" Often, the response given to the hypothetical question is the reason the suspect committed the crime or lied about it.

QUESTION TYPES

Question types discussed in this section will be a review of Chapter 4, while others will be new types of questions that are specific to the interrogation.

Enticement Question

An enticement question is a non-accusatory question designed to elicit a specific behavior or response from the suspect. It is used when the suspect has already given his account of the incident. You offer evidence that contradicts the suspect's story. It often forces a suspect to change his original story. For example, if the suspect says that he did not steal the money from the register and he did not work the register on the day in question, you might say, "Is there any reason we would have a video showing you on the register that day?" This might cause the suspect to change his story and admit that he had been on the register. You could then respond, "Is there any reason a video might show you taking money?" and the interrogation would continue. You may or may not actually have a video showing the suspect taking the money. Here, you did not say you have video, you only asked if there was a reason one might show the suspect doing something. Note that, in some states, it is not legal to indicate you have evidence when you do not in an interrogation setting.

You should not let the suspect know if you have the evidence. If questioned about the evidence, reply that the information cannot be revealed at this stage of the investigation. Also, be cautious not to suggest a piece of evidence that could not possibly exist. For example, if the suspect has been taking things from his employer by concealing items in the restroom, you would not mention that an eyewitness saw him because it is highly unlikely there would be a witness in the privacy of a restroom stall. You must also be cautious when designing a question when there is an obvious alternative reason for the proposed evidence. For example, you might ask, "Is there a reason your fingerprints may have been found on the gun?" to which the suspect responds, "Yeah, because it is my gun."

Reflective Question

A reflective question is a form of reflective listening. You reflect back what the suspect has previously said or done. For example, if in response to a question the suspect says, "I do not feel comfortable discussing it now," you might say, "I understand that you don't feel comfortable now, do you want to take a minute and think about it?" or "It's understandable you feel uncomfortable talking about it, but you'll feel better if put your feelings into words." This can help bring the suspect around.

Redirection Question

A redirection question is used to redirect the conversation when it veers off-topic or is going nowhere. This occurs when the suspect does not want to cooperate, talk or creates a distraction by getting off-topic. You can redirect the suspect by saying, "Getting back to the day the crime occurred last Saturday night, where were you?"

Ego-Boosting Question

An ego-boosting question is designed to boost the suspect's ego. It can be used in collaboration with the "Cooperation with the Suspect" technique mentioned in the previous section. When using this type of question, you are attempting to enlist the suspect as an ally. You want to dispel any perception that the suspect will be judged based on his behavior. You can also use this question to alleviate the suspect's feelings of guilt. You may say, "You are an honest person, aren't you?"

Provocative Question

This question is generally used in reference to the suspect's defense mechanisms and nervous behavior. You point out the suspect's defense mechanisms or nervous behavior and inquire about the source. You do this to gain information and deal with the negative behavior in a constructive way. You do not want to create a power struggle or adversarial situation. You may use this type of question to enhance tension to see the suspect's verbal and nonverbal behavior. This technique can be risky and care should be taken to ensure that it is conducted in a positive and constructive manner. The goal is to understand a suspect's discomfort and to inquire as to its origin.

Leading Question

Leading questions are questions that imply the desired answer. Leading questions were first introduced in Chapter 4 as improper in the interview process. The interview is used to gather information and, therefore, the interviewer generally does not want to ask leading questions.

By the time the interrogation occurs, you have already obtained the information you need, and you use that information to obtain an admission or confession from the suspect. Consequently, you may ask leading questions during the interrogation because you already know the answer to the question. An example of a leading question is, "You were at John's house last Saturday night, right?" This type of question implies that you are looking for a truthful response. It results in greater cooperation from the suspect, increases rapport, and helps keep the suspect engaged in the interrogation.

Expansion-Probing Question

An expansion-probing question requires the suspect to build upon their last answer. It is a tactful way you cause the suspect to continue talking. Rather than accusing the suspect of withholding information, you ask questions that imply more information is expected. For example, instead of saying, "Is that all?" you would say, "What else is there?"

DECEPTION

A Strong Word of Caution

Call it lie detection, mind reading, or whatever, there are certain things that the mind and body do that give us some indication of what the suspect is thinking. Much of it is based on science and the experience of psychologists and investigators. However, though much of this information has been tested and researched, most will agree that it is hardly an exacting science. In fact, there are credible studies that suggest that investigators trained in deception detection are no better at predicting deception than random chance. Ultimately, when a person is stressed, they will exhibit certain signs. Lying, deceiving and fear of detection all cause stress. It is critical to understand this sequence since the person experiencing stress may or may not be deceiving or fear consequences of their actions - it may be for other reasons.

Practice and common sense should play a major role its use.

Most of the signs that will be discussed are based on the "flight or fight" response of humans (this will be discussed more in Physiological Aspects below). This is based on perception, and as such, an actual threat is not to a person's life but to something very important to that person such as his freedom (such as incarceration, etc.). The person is in a narrow state of mind and the body reacts in some dramatic ways.

It is these manifestations that can lead to the detection of deceptive behavior. The greater the fear of detection, the greater the probability that the suspect will exhibit verbal and nonverbal behavior that is incongruent with their baseline, discussed below. The incongruency is often made without the suspect even knowing it. In general, the stronger the emotion, the greater the likelihood of the incongruency.

It is important to examine the consistency of deceptive behavior as it relates to a specific topic or issue. This can be done through clever trial and error. If you see behavior that is new (not connected before to any other topic or issue) you can return to the topic that caused the behavior and continue to ask questions designed to test for that behavior again.

Deception is the state of being deceived or misled. Accordingly, you must be able to recognize and manage deception. This section of the book addresses verbal and nonverbal signs of deception. A person's reactions can give you some indication of what the suspect is thinking.

DEVELOPING A BASELINE

At the beginning of the interrogation, you ask a series of control questions to establish a baseline of the suspect's normal behavior. Baseline refers to how the suspect interacts under normal circumstances in a non-threatening environment. It is used as a basis for measuring his behavior during the interrogation. It allows you to identify when the suspect is exhibiting deceptive behavior. The reasoning behind establishing a baseline is that all people behave differently, therefore for you to identify deceptive behavior, you must be able to identify non-deceptive behavior.

To establish a baseline, the suspect should be comfortable. While engaging in non-threatening conversation, you note the suspect's body language: how he normally sits, speaks, and gestures. You are looking for what is average or usual for that person. It is important to note if the suspect uses a lot of hand gestures, has a natural crackle in his voice, licks his lips a lot, or touches his face and hands excessively. These may be normal behavior for this person even though they are generally signs of deception. These are behaviors that might otherwise be interpreted as signs of deception if not identified during the baseline assessment.

The baseline assessment can be conducted during the rapport building stage of the interrogation. It is conducted without the knowledge of the suspect. It is an informal identification of the suspect's communication style under normal circumstances. As you engage in rapport building conversation discussed in the previous chapter, you are making mental notes of the suspect's verbal and nonverbal responses. These are non-stressful control questions.

As you begin to feel that rapport is established, you will gradually direct the conversation to the event in question by asking the suspect to describe the time frame just before the event occurred. For example, if the event occurred at work, the suspect will be asked to describe what he did before work, how he got there, and how his shift began. Typically, the description is about non-stressful, day-to-day activities. You observe the suspect during this time to help further develop a baseline.

Next, you ask an open-ended question about the actual event in question. As the suspect provides a narrative response, you observe his verbal and nonverbal communication. Discrepancies with his baseline assessment may indicate deception.

Another approach that can be used is to ask the suspect to recall the crime or event in reverse order. This is generally done after the suspect has given a narrative account of the event. In this technique, you prompt the suspect to explain specific parts of the event beginning with the end. Discussing the event in reverse order requires tapping into "real" memory. It is much harder for a person to remember a falsified story using this technique because the fabrication is not from "real" memory, and therefore contradictions and signs of stress will be evident. The contradictions can later be used against the suspect. Occasionally, the suspect might recall the truth from actual "real" memory without even realizing it.

You may have the suspect describe the event a third time. This time, you are looking for behavior clusters, which will be discussed in the next section.

It is important to note that baseline can actually change during the interrogation. As the suspect becomes tired, frustrated or fearful, if you stray into different topics or if other dynamics change then baseline and incongruencies can change as well. Be flexible and attentive to how these might change.

Signs of Deception

One sign of deception is when the suspect's verbal and nonverbal behaviors are incongruent with their baseline behaviors. For example, the suspect may say that he did not steal the money, yet at the same time, he begins to sweat profusely. The incongruence will increase and be more obvious as the suspect's fear of detection increases. Usually, the suspect is unaware of the incongruence of their verbal and nonverbal behavior.

Deceptive behavior may be related to a side issue unrelated to, or unimportant to, the events relevant to the interrogation. Therefore, it is important to examine the consistency of deceptive behavior as it relates to a specific topic or issue. This can be done through attentive trial and error. If a new behavior is observed, you note what topic generated that behavior and then return to that subject and continue to ask questions designed to test for that behavior again.

Negative Clusters

As you begin to observe signs of deception, you look for behavior to occur in clusters. Remember, deceptive behavior is defined as behavior that is inconsistent with behavior observed in the baseline assessment. You look for a cluster of five different deceptive responses to any question or issue; this is a sign of deception. Only a few deceptive behaviors are not enough. Adhering to five signs helps reduce the chance that deception is being misinterpreted. As a note, there are credible studies that show properly trained interrogators are not able to detect deception beyond mere chance. This is very important when trying to assess deception from regular/normal behavior alone. Also, be aware that truthful behaviors come in clusters too, for example, comfortable body position, maintaining good eye contact, etc.

Verbal Signals

Verbal signs of deception refer to ways the suspect lies to you when answering questions. The common examples listed below refer to the suspect's baseline. It is not necessary for the suspect to display all the examples. The key to a successful interrogation is to understand what signals the suspect may be sending.

How a Suspect Says "No"

How a person says "no" can be important. Exhibiting any of the following traits while saying "no" can be a sign of deception:

- Too friendly when saying "no."
- Shifting their body after answering with a "no."
- Crossing legs when saying "no."
- Looking away when saying "no."
- Shuttering eyes (blinking a lot) when saying "no."
- Shaking head when saying "no."
- Biting lips when saying "no."
- Appearance of insincerity when saying "no."
- Hesitate before answering when saying "no."
- A breathless "no."
- Appearing thoughtful or too casual when saying "no."
- Eyes directed somewhere else when saying "no."

- Blank stare while answering when saying "no."
- Saying "no" many times in rapid succession.

Moods

Moods indicate deception when they change after a specific question is asked. Lying creates stress, changes in mood can indicate an increase in stress, and therefore, changes in mood or other nuances may indicate deception. Response states that indicate changes in mood include:

- Anger.
- Swearing - attacking the interviewer, the victim, or case facts.
- Depression.
- Comments about emotional problems, depression, or insomnia; any statement about personal life problems (family, health); statements about punishments the suspect may receive because of investigation.

Use of Rationalizing Words

Using rationalizing words such as "almost, sort of, possibly."

Information Offered By the Suspect

If a suspect offers additional information to support their denial, it may be a sign of deception. This includes untimely explanations that were not asked for or are premature or excuses for things that implicate the suspect. Honest people will respond simply that they did not do it. The untruthful tend to expand and elaborate.

The Overly Polite

You should be suspicious of a suspect who is overly polite or too helpful; this is a red flag for deception. The suspect uses these tactics to get you to like him. He may also be trying to find out what you know and what direction the interrogation is going. He then might try to direct you away from him and to something or someone else.

Delay Tactics

Responses to your questions: There are several different types of delay tactics a suspect may use to buy time. He may ask you to repeat a question as a delay tactic while he considers a response that will get him off the hook. He may respond to a question with a question, to avoid having to answer the question. He mat avoid questions, only answer a portion of it or skipping over important time frames in the answer. He may tell you that he does not understand or does not know what he is trying to communicate.

Accusations: The most common delay tactic is, “Are you accusing me of this?” This breaks the flow of the interrogation.

Redirection: The suspect may also redirect the conversation or topic to another less significant or stressful topic. When using this tactic, the suspect is attempting to direct you elsewhere to avoid having to tell a lie, for example, “Why would I steal from the company?” This avoids having to lie about the actual culpability in this scenario.

Shifting or lessening blame: Another delay tactic is when the suspect tries to shift blame to others or provide possible alternative explanations for why the crime or violation took place, for example, “Maybe it was really an accident”, “The person who did it could have been anybody,” or “That evidence can be interpreted many other ways.”

Selective attention to details: Another way to delay the interrogations is paying too much attention to little, irrelevant details or evading relevant, perhaps incriminating details by only discussing overall issues.

Deep thought: In the most extreme type of delay tactic, the suspect is involved in such deep internal thought, such as just before making an admission or confession, that he did not even hear your question.

Memory Lapses: Delays occur when the suspect indicates that there are memory lapses, e.g. “I don’t really remember.”

Stalling: A suspect can delay by laughing, coughing, or asking to repeat questions.

Statements that Lack Emotion

This is a sign the statement is fabricated, or the suspect is refusing to face the hurtful part of the event, or perhaps to appear unaffected.

Throwing You a Bone

"Throwing you a bone" refers to when the suspect concedes to an element of the crime but the concession is not totally accurate. It is rare that the first admission from a suspect is completely truthful. To have you believe he is being truthful, the suspect will admit to something small, for example, he might admit to taking $10 when in fact the figure was much more than that. This is in a sense a compromise on the part of the suspect and is a sign that he is close to confessing.

Pointing Out Truthful or Cooperative Behavior

The suspect may point out how cooperative or truthful he has been in the past as a means of delaying answering the question. This is a sign that deception is taking place.

Moral or Honest Exclamations

If the suspect begins making exclamations about his morals or honesty, it may be a sign of deception. The suspect will say things like, “I swear to God” or “My father is a police officer/priest/etc., and he will vouch for me”. The suspect may use other exaggerated phrases like, “honestly, truthfully!”

Recollection – Truth or Lie

You can recognize deception based on how the suspect recalls the details of the event. People who are truthful will tell a story with only minor changes. The untruthful suspect needs to have an excellent memory to maintain all aspects of a series of lies they have created. This is why it is good to get specifics about many aspects of a story, especially minor details. You should have the suspect reaffirm these details and ask questions rapidly so the suspect does not have enough time to make up a well-thought-out answer. Watch closely for deceptive/stressful behavior while doing this.

The Suspect Giving In

If a suspect "gives in" it is a sign of deception. The innocent do not generally admit guilt or offer to pay for the crime or act. The guilty do. A suspect who gives in might say, "I'll confess if it will make you happy" or "If I just pay for the theft, will you let me go?" If this happens, you corroborate the confession to be assured that you have the right person. There are cases though where persons being interrogated will confess even if they are innocent, just to get out of what may be for them a very stressful situation.

Nonverbal Signals

The following section will discuss nonverbal signals of deception. Most of the signs discussed in this section are based on the "fight or flight" response of humans. This is a primitive physiological response to a threat or perceived threat in which the sympathetic nervous system initiates physiological changes such as increased heart rate. This physiological response is based on the perception of a threat. The physiological changes may indicate stress and can then lead to the detection of deceptive behavior.

Throughout this section, it is important to keep in mind how your nonverbal behavior signals can affect a suspect's nonverbal signs of deception. If a suspect thinks you believe him, he may become comfortable and therefore will not show signs of stress. An innocent person may not think you believe them and may exhibit stressful behavior because they are nervous about being interrogated. This illustrates the importance of understanding the suspect's true state when making assessments of deception.

You should be careful about pointing out a suspect's nonverbal behavior because he may then alter his behavior to better hide his deception. Nonverbal clues are harder to conceal than verbal clues. There is no one single behavior that will absolutely indicate deception on the part of the suspect. As previously noted, you look for clusters of five different behaviors from the same stimuli, such as a statement of fact about the case. If a given stimulus consistently generates the same deceptive behavior, you cross-reference it against verbal clues to help determine if the suspect is lying. You may keep simple notes regarding the observed behavior without drawing the suspect's attention. This will help you remember what behavior was exhibited earlier in the interrogation.

Factors that affect nonverbal behaviors will be discussed in this section. They are proxemics, psychological aspects, memory, and specific body parts. Nonverbal indicators are the most useful in detecting deception although they are more difficult to read and interpret than verbal signals.

Proxemics

Proxemics is the examination of differences in personal space based on cultural, behavioral, and sociological aspects. This refers to the comfort zones discussed in Chapter 4. Your position in relation to the suspect can cause discomfort or comfort as the emotions and general atmosphere dictate. The interrogation is a more intense interaction than the interview, therefore, you can use the comfort zones to manage the intensity.

There may be times when you will want to move in and out of these zones. For example, when the suspect becomes emotional, such as when he may be confessing, it may help to move from the social to the personal zone to help establish more of a compassionate and personal rapport. You may also manage stress levels either to increase or to decrease the levels to assist with judging nonverbal deceptive behavior. However, intruding into a suspect's personal space has its risk. Considerations of safety, harassment, false imprisonment or unwanted advances may dictate a different approach.

Physiological Aspects

People will exhibit certain nonverbal signs of stress based largely on what is happening with their nervous system. The autonomic nervous system is primarily subconscious and, as such, is beyond the control of the conscious mind. It controls the heart, smooth muscles (such as blood vessels), and internal glands and organs. Therefore, many of the nonverbal signs of deception will be exhibited without conscious intent (or knowledge) on the part of the suspect.

The important part of the autonomic nervous system is the sympathetic nervous system. This inhibits certain functions, thus preparing the body for a stressful situation. Peripheral blood flow is constricted, causing blood flow to the skin to decrease and overall blood flow to the heart and muscles to increase to help the body prepare for "flight or fight." Adrenaline is released and blood sugar levels are increased. Heart rate and breathing rate are increased to allow more blood and oxygen into the system. Feet and hands start to sweat to help cool the body. These things occur in an individual who is experiencing fear or anger. The suspect will exhibit these behaviors as he fears detection of his lie or as he anticipates the consequences of his actions.

Memory

Persons who are deceptive experience more memory lapses than others. This can be due to repression, which is when the person has hidden the event from conscious thought. It can also be because the suspect is too emotional to discuss it. Very often, it is an intentional memory loss. Intentional memory loss prevents the suspect from having to lie about the central issue of the question of his guilt. This type of memory lapse shows the highest probability of deception. It is likely that the suspect will remember something if asked a fact about the event, such as, "Earlier you said you got into the house through the window. Was it open or closed?" If you ask about one important fact, other relevant facts will come up with it. The probability that these types of questions will produce memory is high, making the assertion by the suspect that he does not remember that much more unbelievable.

Deceptive Body Signs of The Head

The head is the easiest part of the body to control and consequently will be where the suspect exhibits and practices the most deceptive behavior. Deceptive body signs related to the head can be classified into three groups: the position of the head, facial expressions, and behaviors.

The actual position of the head can yield valuable information.

Head Tilted

If the head is tilted, the suspect is probably listening.

Remains Straight

If the head remains straight, the suspect may be angry.

Chin Hits Chest

If the chin hits the chest, held down, this could be a sign of depression or resignation. If the suspect rests his head in his hands, it may mean the suspect is thinking about what is being said and it may be an indication of internal dialog.

Hands Form Pyramid

If the person forms a pyramid with his hands, it can be an indication that he feels superior.

Thinker Pose

The "thinker" pose, one or both elbows on the knee, fists on the chin or forehead, means the person is probably faking that he is paying attention. He may be trying to think around the topic.

Resting Head in Hands

If the suspect rests his head in his hands, this is a sign that the suspect may be depressed or that he is beginning to accept what he is experiencing, such as being ready to confess or make an admission.

Rolling of the Head

People who are being untruthful roll their heads to stretch tense neck muscles. The movements will be quick and jerky.

Head Titled Down

The head may tilt face down, which is a showing of a submissive attitude. The head tilted back shows arrogance sometimes exhibited by the suspect, who is trying to elevate himself above the act or crime in question.

Facial expressions involve all parts of the face: the mouth, eyes, nose, and complexion.

Smiles

The type of smile a suspect uses can mean different things. If a person smiles and uses their mouth, it is a good sign that the person is truthful. If he only shows the upper teeth in the smile, this is a sign the suspect feels in control of the situation. Certain muscles in the face, especially around the mouth and eyes, are controlled involuntarily by genuine emotion. Therefore, it is difficult to fake a smile that appears sincere.

An overly concerned pleasant look on the suspect's face is a sign of false interest or disguised concern or fear.

Flushing in Face

Flushing in the face, which is the result of the body forcing blood onto the larger muscles and torso due to the stress response, is an indication of fear. Redness in the face is a sign of anger due to increased blood pressure.

Eyes and Lips Become Darker

The eyes and lips may become darker as stress is experienced due to a lack of oxygen in these areas.

Freezing Face

A suspect may "freeze" his face to hide what is really going on inside. This is a good sign the suspect is being deceitful. By watching other parts of the body when this happens, you may see signs of deception because, as the suspect consciously concentrates on faking facial expressions, he may unknowingly exhibit behavior from other parts of the body. This is known as behavior leakage.

Facial Twitches

Facial twitches, usually between ¼ to ½ second in duration, are signs the suspect is experiencing stress.

Itch, Pick At, or Stroke Nose

During periods of stress, as blood pressure in the nose (the most sensitive part of the body to stress) increases or drops, the tissue in the nose will become irritated, causing the suspect to itch, stroke, or pick at it. In fact, watch for touching of this entire area (nose, mouth, and chin). Deceptive people will touch this area more often than truthful people.

Inappropriate Facial Gestures or Faked Emotions

A suspect may use emotion to deceive you, for example, to appear to cry for the victim when he is really crying about the fact that he is close to being discovered. In addition to smiles, quick, surprised-sounding laughs or inappropriate smirks are a sign of a person who is insincere or deceptive.

Carotid Artery

The carotid artery, located on either side of the throat, will often pulse visibly and the Adam's apple will shake a bit when a suspect experiences stress.

Eye Blinking

A change in the amount of eye blinking observed during the baseline may be a sign of how fast the suspect is thinking. If the eyelids stay closed for longer than normal, this could be a sign of stress or an indication that the suspect does not want to look at you. A decrease in the amount of blinking can be a sign that the person is having an intense internal dialogue, perhaps weighing whether or not to confess. It may reflect an increase in interest in what you are talking about. When people are nervous, they squint, glance up, and stare more than usual.

Certain behaviors associated with the head will also reveal signs of deception.

Eyeglasses

A person who wears glasses may push them up on the nose as the glasses slide down the bridge of the nose. This can be an effort to hide the eyes. It can also be because the suspect has been sweating more, causing the glasses to slide more than usual.

Yawning

Yawning can mean several things. It may be because the suspect needs more oxygen due to the emotional demands of interrogation questioning. Yawning can also be used to feign disinterest or to buy time. The suspect might yawn because he is actually tired or bored with the interview. It is important to keep in mind the time of day or night and the duration of the interrogation.

Pace of Breathing

Breathing can also reveal information about deception. An untruthful person will breathe more rapidly (more than 18 to 22 times a minute) than a truthful person will. In addition, the upper chest will become tense and the suspect's inhaling and exhaling will not be full. The breathing will be shallow and not smooth, causing the suspect to gasp and sigh occasionally.

Several behaviors associated with the mouth are indicative of deception.

Hiding the Mouth

Attempting to hide the mouth may be a subconscious attempt to stop the mouth from what it is saying. This could manifest itself as a hand or finger over the mouth, putting a pen or pair of glasses to the lips, or biting nails. Biting or pursing of the lips is another sign of stress.

Dry-Mouth

Dry-mouth is a very common signal of deception because stress causes the mouth to produce less saliva and as the suspect talks, the mouth will make a tacky or clicking sound. He will try to wet his now dry lips and swallow more often. He will also ask for water more often.

Eye Contact

On average, people maintain eye contact 40-60% of the time they are conversing. Too much or too little eye contact can be a sign of deception. Eye contact can be tricky to interpret properly. If a suspect does not maintain eye contact, it does not necessarily imply deception. Cultural and other social norms may affect the amount of eye contact a person makes. The suspect's normal eye contact habits should be observed during the baseline assessment. If you notice that the suspect's level of eye contact changes during the interrogation, it can mean several things. Too much eye contact can be an attempt to appear truthful or interested. It can also mean the suspect is watching you for some indication of how you are reacting. Some suspects will try to avoid your attempts to see the behavior showing in his eyes by looking at other things, such as nails or hands. He may cover his face with his hand, close his eyes, or nonchalantly look at anything but you.

Deceptive Body Signs of The Arms

The arms are another good source of deceptive body language.

Shrugging, Dropping, Hunching, or Pulling Back Shoulders

A shrug from the shoulders is a sign of denial, while dropping or hunching of the shoulders is an indication of depression or acceptance. Pulling the shoulders back while tightening the neck can be a sign of anger.

Elbows Pull In

When a suspect is relaxed and does not feel threatened, the elbows hang loose to the side of the body. However, when a suspect is stressed or threatened, he will subconsciously try to protect vital areas. The elbows will pull in to cover the torso and the groin. A movement of any part of the body to protect the abdominal area, such as crossing the legs or hunching the legs up close to the chest, can be a sign of this protective behavior.

Hugs Self

If the suspect hunches over and hugs himself, this can be a sign of self-reassurance as he experiences loss or depression. Propping the head up with the hands can indicate disinterest. In this situation, the body is slumped because the suspect is tired and needs to support his head.

Crossing Arms, Clenching Fists

If a suspect crosses his arms and clenches his fists under their arms, this person is probably angry. If, in the same posture, he grabs his arms, this may be a sign that the suspect will not easily change his mind.

Hand Gestures

Excessive use of hand gestures is sometimes considered a nervous response. However, certain cultures use many hand gestures to accent words. Also, those who are not very good with verbal skills tend to use their hands more to help them communicate adequately. The suspect's normal use of hand gestures should be established during the baseline assessment. If a person is untruthful, his gestures will be jerky due to tense muscles. Furthermore, their gestures will not appear natural and will be timed inappropriately, either too soon or too late.

Hand Gestures to Hide Face

A suspect may be using hand gestures to keep from having to look at you. For example, he will reach to rub his nose and in the process also shield his eyes from your view or cover his face completely.

Reenacting and Event

When a suspect is describing an emotional or significant event, he may visually recreate the event in his mind and "relive" it by gesturing with his hands, such as how the suspect may have struck the victim in an assault. This generally occurs when the suspect is stressed.

Grooming, Picking, Tapping Fingers

An increase in other types of hand movements such as grooming or finger tapping can be a good indication of an increase in stress level. Nervous outlets, such as picking at lint or grooming, are important and should be noted if they occur during the discussion of areas that are making the suspect nervous.

Rubbing, Itching

Excessive rubbing or itching may be a sign of deception. Rubbing or itching of the arms or ears may be an indication of an increase in stress while massaging the back of the neck is a sign of agitation.

Rubbing or Massaging Hands

If a suspect rubs or massages their hands, this can mean that he is trying to comfort himself.

Rubbing Point of Chin

Rubbing the point of the chin with the dominant hand is a sign of acquiescence and the suspect may be ready to make an admission.

Itchiness in Skin

As the blood in the body is diverted to the blood vessels in the skin, this will cause the blood pressure in these areas to increase. This can create an itchy sensation, as this irritates the nerves located in the skin. This is especially true in the upper trunk, nose, and arms. If the suspect sits with his hands open, palms up (arms extended), this can mean that the suspect is opening up.

Fine Motor Skills

Changes in fine motor skills can indicate deceptive behavior. A truthful person has good fine motor coordination; he can gesture and write smoothly and naturally. An untruthful person has illegible or spiky handwriting and his hands are sweaty and clammy, further impacting his writing. This will become evident during a written statement or other writing exemplars.

Deceptive Body Signs of The Legs

The positioning and movement of the legs and feet can provide valuable information regarding deception. The feet are at the extreme end of the body, therefore, people pay the least amount of attention to controlling them.

Sitting Facing Forward, Legs Open

A truthful suspect will sit with his body facing the interviewer with their legs open and relaxed.

Wiggling, Shaking, or Bouncing of the Feet

Wiggling, shaking, or bouncing of the feet, especially if the foot is up off the floor, is an indication of stress.

The Chair

If the suspect slides his feet under the chair, this is a sign of stress, especially if the suspect crosses his legs while doing this.

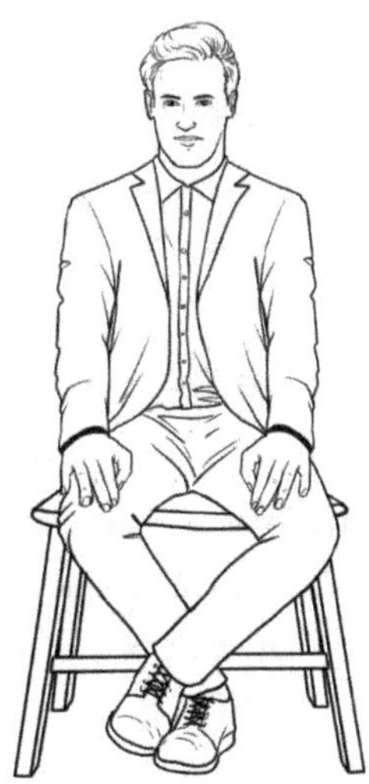

Crossing of the Legs

Extraneous movement in the legs is a sign of increased stress. If the suspect turns and crosses his legs so he is facing away from you, it is a sign of rejection, and conversely, if the legs are open and facing you, it is a sign of acceptance.

Legs Out In Front

If the suspect puts a leg out in front of him, he is maintaining a certain distance between you and himself. If he points a leg toward the door, it means he is ready to leave.

Wiggling or Shaking of the Knees

A wiggling or shaking of the knees is a sign of agitation and increased stress.

Toes

If the toes, while the feet are flat on the floor, point inward, this is a sign of someone who is introverted. If the toes point out, the person may feel comfortable or even superior.

Crossing Legs at the Knee

If a suspect crosses his legs higher up at the knee, this is a more defensive posture than crossing them at the ankle (it protects the abdominal region more).

Remember also that as a truthful person may exhibit these behaviors, it may be because he is merely uncomfortable about being interrogated.

Deceptive Body Signs of Sitting Positions

The sitting position can reveal important information about the suspect.

Ready to Run

If a suspect is sitting as though he were ready to run, leaning to one side with the feet under the weight of the body, it is an indication he is experiencing extreme stress and that he very much wants to leave. He will probably also be facing the door or in a direction away from the interrogator.

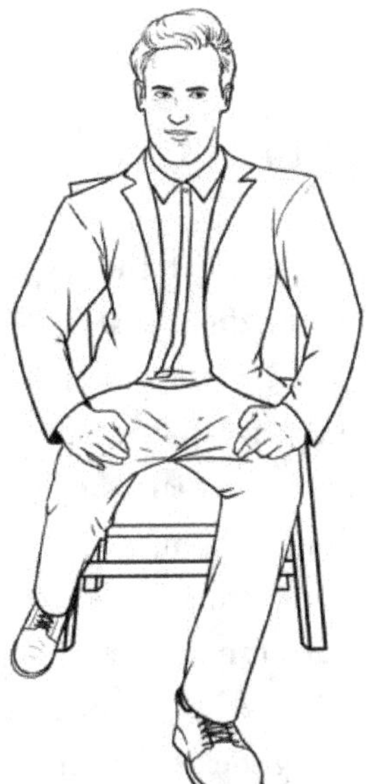

Sitting in the Chair

Some suspects will try to appear macho or overtly bored with the interrogation by sitting in the chair, slouched back with the legs kicked out and hands draped over the side of the chair or tucked into the pants. A suspect may try to distance himself from you by turning the chair around and sitting in it backward. This places more of a barrier between you

and the suspect. A relaxed person will move around and change positions while sitting in a chair.

When an untruthful person sits down in a chair, he will move it first, whereas a truthful person will sit in it without thought. The untruthful person moves the chair at an angle so he does not have to face you. He may also move the chair away from you or sit sideways in the chair, also to keep from having to face you. Both maneuvers can be in an effort to hide and protect the abdominal area. This is an unconscious reaction to protecting vulnerable areas. The abdominal area is vulnerable because it doesn't have any bones protecting it, unlike the upper back and chest.

Freezing the Entire Body

A deceptive person may freeze their body into one position for long periods of time - clenching their fists, maintaining a rigid posture, crossing of legs, and sitting on hands are signs of this. This is like the "frozen" face discussed earlier and may be an effort to hide tensions, agitation, or stress.

DENIAL

Denial is when the suspect claims no involvement in the crime or act. It is a specific and distinct state of the interrogation, of which you should be particularly aware. It is the phase of the interrogation when the suspect denies he committed the act in question. He is probably also in denial about the severity of the offense. Denial usually occurs after an accusation has been made or during rationalization, which will be discussed later in this chapter. Denial may also occur during the development of the admission or confession. When this occurs, it may be an honest denial or the suspect may be attempting to further minimize his actions. During an interrogation, you stop the suspect from making the denial (in contrast to what is done during an interview). You allow the suspect to speak his denial. This section will discuss the suspect, how he will be thinking when making a denial, and what impact you can have on the denial. In addition, different types of denial will be discussed, and what you should do when denial continues.

Reasons for Denial

You must always keep in mind a suspect's reasons for being in denial. The art of getting around the denial is to offer a rationalization that minimizes the offense and, therefore, reduces the stigma attached to it. Rationalizations are based on the suspect's own value system, and they are established early in the interrogation. If the wrong rationalization is selected, it may not work.

As an example, if you try to suggest the suspect took the money for financial reasons, this would not work if the suspect did not need money. Perhaps he took the money for purposes of revenge, or maybe your suspect is mentally ill. The end result its that the suspect will not respond if this is match his reason for denial.

When using rationalizations, it is wise to use third person and hypothetical situations initially. This way, you can suggest several rationalizations as general reasons people commit the act in question without committing to one rationalization for the suspect. If the suspect exhibits stressful behavior or signs of deception when a certain rationalization is mentioned, it might be the right one.

Break it Down

Denial is more likely to occur when the suspect is presented with the offense in its entirety. Therefore, it is more effective to break the offense down and approach small issues one at a time. This makes the perceived consequences less formidable, and you can connect the dots later for bigger issues. Several small admissions can be combined to draw a larger conclusion, reducing the probability of inaccurate denials.

Confrontation and the Suspect

If you are too confrontational with the suspect, especially in the early stages of the interrogation, it will increase the likelihood of a strong denial. Similarly, using a strong word, for example, "steal" rather than "take", increases the likelihood of denial.

Some suspects will try to bait you into accusing because he wants to force a denial and wait for the first chance to do so. Many will raise the issue of their guilt so that he can deny it. You may choose to avoid the issue of the suspect's guilt, thus avoiding the dilemma of having to establish guilt when it has not been established to your satisfaction. If a suspect does try to force a denial, you can respond by moving the discussion in another direction. For example, if the suspect says, "Are you accusing me of ...?" You can respond, "We can discuss that later. In the meantime, I need to cover some other issues." You move the topic to another area without appearing to evade the question; however, if not done adequately, this may lead the suspect to believe you are not confident in his guilt.

Waiting too long to pose an assumptive question can also result in denial. If the suspect reaches the state in which he feels he should confess, you must utilize that opportunity. Otherwise, he may regain his emotional strength and start to believe that a denial might be successful. However, you must be cautious not to ask an assumptive question too soon. If he is not ready, it will only cause a denial. The more a person denies, the more he locks himself in and the more he will believe you are buying his denials. If a suspect does make a denial, you reassert your beliefs so that the suspect maintains a belief in your credibility and confidence in his guilt.

TYPES OF DENIAL

There are several types of denial you will encounter. You will respond to the suspect based on the type of denial. Therefore, you must be able to identify the type of denial the suspect is making.

Truthful

A truthful denial is where the suspect makes a denial because he is not culpable. Your knowledge of the facts of the case, ability to gauge deceptive behavior, and willingness to be receptive to new information are all very important in establishing whether a denial is true or not. With any denial, you must remember that you may have the wrong person. Truthful denials involve a person who maintains good eye contact and interrupts immediately upon any accusation. The assertion is natural and all behaviors are appropriate in amount, timing, and in type and are consistent with baseline behaviors. The denials of an innocent suspect will increase with time while the guilty will begin to fade in intensity.

General

Some suspects will make a very general denial, for example, "I haven't done anything wrong". When this occurs, it will usually occur early in the interrogation. Other suspects will wait until there is an opportunity.

Direct

A direct denial refers to a suspect who makes a strong denial right away. When a suspect makes a strong and direct denial, he may shake his head "no", while picking his eyebrows and making direct eye contact with you. In this type of denial, the suspect will try to interrupt you to make his denial. For example, he might say, "Excuse me," or "May I say something?" When this occurs, you can stop the denial by using the person's first name. People are conditioned to stop and listen, at least for a moment when they hear their name. Then, to keep the suspect from leaving and to keep his interest piqued, you tell him that you will be discussing some important information and that he will need to make some important decisions. This is neutral and noncommittal. It does not imply you have any evidence or even that the suspect is guilty. In fact, you may have no intention of saying anything to the suspect about the facts of the case. This is merely a method of stopping the denial and moving the conversation to another topic.

Optimally, you will now move to rationalization. You can also tell the suspect he will have a chance to talk later when you are finished. Hopefully, by this point, the rationalizations will have taken effect and he will have made an admission.

In a direct denial, you can also allow the suspect to make his denial. Then, after the suspect has made his denial, you say, “Is there anything else?” or "Are you finished?" and then you move with resolve back to what was being said before the interruption. When this happens, the suspect will believe that you did not believe his denial.

When a suspect begins to make a direct denial, you can stop him and make the denial for him. You then proceed to tell him that people usually deny involvement but that his denial does not match the facts of the investigation. You might also tell him that it is better to say nothing at all than to lie.

Another approach you might use is to increase your rate of speech, speech volume, and pitch when you sense the suspect is going to make a direct denial. This has the effect of telling the suspect that what you are about to say is important, thus lessening his desire to interrupt to make a denial. It is more difficult for a person to interrupt someone who appears intent on what they are saying.

Finally, you can use body language to dismiss a direct denial. For example, you can turn your head, break eye contact, or hold up your hand, palm out. These actions, taken together, tell the suspect that you are not paying attention to what he is saying. If you give the suspect the impression you have heard and believe the denial, he will think there is a chance you believe him. This will be a barrier when you try to further get an admission or a confession; the suspect will only strengthen his resolve.

Indirect

An indirect denial is when a suspect doesn’t specifically deny the offense, but indirectly maintains his innocence. When this occurs, it is helpful to move to rationalization. This type of suspect is closer to confession than a suspect who makes a direct denial. Indirect denials include dropping names or describing himself as religious. The suspect might say, “I wouldn’t need to do that,” or “That is not possible”. In this situation, the suspect does not specifically deny but distracts to an indirect way of maintaining innocence and truthfulness. Rationalizations used with an indirect denial must work for that suspect. A proper response to the indirect denial is to acknowledge the denial. For example, if the suspect says, "I couldn't have done that," you might say, "Good, that is one more reason you'll want to help me clear this up." In this scenario, you use the denial against the suspect.

If Denial Continues

As the interrogation progresses and the suspect continues to make denials, you can begin showing disbelief at the suspect's unwillingness to cooperate. You may throw up you hands, stand up, and turn around to express displeasure at the suspect's inability to help connect. You reinforce this by saying, "I know you want to get this straightened out!" You might tell the suspect to himself in your shoes. What would he do?

You can also illustrate your frustration. You say, "I'm not wearing a watch" when both you and the suspect can see that you are wearing a watch. You then say, "Ask me if I'm wearing a watch." The suspect reluctantly says, "Okay, are you wearing a watch?" You then deny it. "No, I'm not wearing a watch." You go on to explain that this is like the investigation. What the suspect is saying does not match the evidence. When using this type of scenario, you avoid specifics, just indicate that the suspect's story does not match the investigation. Otherwise, the suspect may try to deny and disprove each piece of evidence you mention.

DENIALS OVER TIME

An untruthful suspect's denials will get weaker over time, whereas the truthful person's denials will get stronger.

Voice Pitch, Volume, and Rate

As denial continues over time, you will notice changes in the suspect's voice pitch, volume, and rate. The pitch of the voice will rise when a person is under stress, especially compared to the baseline. If you ask a question designed to invoke stress in a person who is guilty, the voice pitch will rise. The same question put to an innocent person probably would not cause this change unless this person is reacting to some other issue.

The voice volume can increase or decrease as a response to stress depending on the emotion the person is feeling. Anger causes a rise and depression causes a drop in volume compared to the baseline.

It is also important to notice changes in voice rate. If the speech slows down, the suspect is probably thinking about what is happening, how to act, and what to say. Speed may also increase as a suspect becomes enthusiastic about proving his lies.

Sighs

Sighs can reveal information about how a suspect is feeling. If a person sighs a lot, he is probably experiencing depression. One or a few sighs is a sign of acceptance, perhaps submission to the reality that he has been caught.

Speech Problems

Speech problems will begin to occur when the suspect is stressed. This happens because when a person is stressed, their mind will often have many thought processes going on at once, each competing for attention. As this occurs, other speech problems arise. Simple words like "the,' "and," or "is" may be omitted. The suspect may also leave off ends of words such as "ing,' "ed," "es". As well, he may stop mid-sentence or repeat words.

The Voice May Crack Under Stress

Persons under stress will slur or stutter more than those not under stress. He will also use more "ummms... ahhhs... eh hems" as well as groans and grunts. Suspects often use these tactics to stall for time while considering what to say.

DENIAL CLUES

Generally, suspects offer clues before making a denial. If you recognize these clues, you can often derail the denial before it occurs or you can prepare yourself for the pending denial. The following is a collection of verbal and nonverbal clues that relate to a suspect's denials. These can help you determine what rationalization will be effective with the suspect. Rationalization will be covered in greater detail later in the chapter.

Impressing with Their Character

The suspect may try to impress you with his character. When this occurs, the suspect will qualify their statements with words or phrases that accentuate their good character. For example, the suspect might say, "honestly," "to tell you the truth," or "really," to accept what he is about to say. It can be an effort to further impress you with his innocence.

Noncommittal Statements

When a suspect makes a noncommittal statement, he refrains from saying anything definite. He may say things that allow him to change his story later. These are generally qualifiers such as, "I almost did it," "I may have done it," "I hardly ever do that," or "It's possible that I did do that." With these types of statements, the suspect can later change his story without being accused of lying.

The Hypothetical

Suspects may use hypothetical situations as a means of gauging your position or where the investigation is going. For example, a suspect might say, "If I had a friend who did this, what would you do to them?"

Avoiding the Situation by Elevation Above It

A suspect may try to elevate himself above the event or the parties involved by using words or phrases that objectify or negatively exaggerate them. For example, he may refer to the other parties, not as friends, but as suspects. Or, he may refer to a slap as an assault. Here, the suspect is trying to appear superior to the other people involved or to the event itself.

Errors in Recollection

If a suspect makes errors when recalling the event, it may be a sign of denial. An error in recollection would include using the present tense to describe a past event. If this occurs, the implication may be that he is making it up as he goes along.

For example, when recalling the events, the suspect says, "And now he is holding the gun to his head." Usually, when people recall an event, they use the past tense, however, there are always exceptions. The suspect's usual way of recalling a past event would be noted during the baseline assessment.

This can also occur in reverse. If the suspect describes an event (while lying) in the present tense and then shifts to the past tense, he may be discussing that part as it really happened, as he describes it unknowingly from memory. For example, the suspect may be asked to describe the event as if it were occurring now. If, while describing the event in the present tense, he unknowingly shifts to past tense (as he recalls from memory), he may say, "Then I hold the gun to his head."

Stalling

Suspects can try to stall as a means of regaining a logical train of thought. Laughter, coughing, or a false yawn, especially if they are out of place, are signs of stalling.

Attacking the Interrogator's Question

This refers to a suspect who identifies a part of your question as incorrect rather than answering the question directly. Deceptive individuals will emphasize the parts of a question that are wrong, whereas truthful suspects will just answer the question as a whole. For example, if you ask, "Did you enter the home by the back door?" The suspect may respond, "No, I didn't enter the home by the BACK door."

Selective Information

Deceptive individuals will be selective about the information provided. Generally, he will give only factual information that cannot be specifically disproved and will admit only what you can already prove. You should be especially leery of a suspect who can remember specific details that exculpate him from an event that occurred a long time ago. How does he remember it? He may not have, it may be a lie.

Complain to Interrupt

Suspects may complain a lot as a means of interrupting. These complaints occur throughout the interview, whereas truthful persons will usually wait until the interview is over before complaining.

"That's Not What I Said"

Some suspects will claim they did not say what you reported they said. This occurs when you catch a suspect in a lie. The suspect responds by saying that is not what he originally said or, to be even more evasive, the suspect will say that that is not what he meant.

ACCEPTANCE

Acceptance is when the suspect decides to accept the fact that he has been caught and that it is better to cooperate than to continue to deny his involvement in the offense. If you recognize when this transition occurs, it can help determine when it is appropriate to make accusations and begin to develop admissions or confessions. Admissions and confessions will be addressed later in this chapter.

A sign that a suspect is entering the stage of acceptance is when he begins to "mirror" your posture and expressions.

These signs may include the following:

- Loosening the clothing (a tie, a shirt collar) or removing a coat.
- Eye contact improves. The suspect faces you, possibly leaning toward you, and the suspect may uncross his legs.
- The shoulders roll forward and slump.
- The eyes roll back and blinking slows down to match a relaxed mood.
- Sighs, a sincere smile, and crying.

Responding to Signs of Acceptance

Acceptance is a critical part of the interrogation, therefore, the way you respond to signs of acceptance can greatly impact the interrogation. The following is a series of possible actions you might take in response to someone in acceptance. These actions will be expanded in the sections dealing with accusation, rationalization, and admission or confession.

Vary the Speech

Here, you slow your speech and lower your pitch. This will require the suspect to pay closer attention to you. This type of speech is also more conducive to relaxing the suspect and getting further acceptance. Also, you will begin to listen more and talk less.

Proximity with The Suspect

Your proximity to the suspect was discussed in an earlier section of this chapter called "Proxemics". During the beginning of the acceptance stage of the interrogation, it is recommended that you sit just outside the physical reach of the suspect. You should be at an angle to the suspect, which will allow the suspect to move around comfortably. Now, you appear alert, attentive, and ready to listen. As the acceptance progresses, you move closer to the suspect, which reassures him.

As you move closer, it becomes more difficult for the suspect to make certain nonverbal behaviors or gestures. You make this move gradually with design and purpose. However, obviously, if you get too close, the suspect may think you are becoming aggressive, being condescending, or trying to make a sexual advance. Use care and common sense in this regard.

BE CAREFUL WHEN EVALUATING

- Was the suspect looking away or breaking eye contact deliberately or because of a distraction?
- Personal biases towards the suspect can cause you to believe or disbelieve them. If you like the suspect, you are more likely to believe what is said, whereas the opposite may be true if you do not like the suspect.
- Delays in response may not be because the suspect is stalling. The suspect may not have understood the question or may be too embarrassed to ask for clarification. Language barriers may also be an issue, especially with someone who speaks another language.
- A suspect who is trembling may not be doing so for emotional reasons; it may be due to a medical condition (for example, muscular disease).
- Cultural differences can come into play. For example, in some cultures, it is improper to maintain eye contact.

THE DECISION TO CONFESS

A suspect will decide to confess if he feels that it is in their best interest to do so. As with any decision, this is based on how the benefits outweigh the consequences. If confessing offers more consequences than benefits, the person will not confess. As usual, the benefits/consequence will be based on the suspect's perceptions and previous experiences. It is important for you to be aware of the issues that affect the suspect's perception. Some common issues are prosecution, embarrassment, and restitution. These topics are covered in detail in "Rationalizations."

Another issue that may affect the suspect's perception of benefits and consequences is you. You might give off a judgmental persona, causing the suspect to think the consequences may be worse than they need to be. In this situation, the suspect thinks you will seek greater punishment than he might have originally expected. Or the suspect might think you will cause them embarrassment.

A suspect's decision to confess may also be the result of their guilt. Guilt occurs when the suspect begins to feel his personal values conflict. An example of conflicting values is lying and protecting oneself. A suspect may think lying is wrong - this is one of his values. But he also feels the need to protect himself from the consequences of his actions, another value. These two values are now in conflict. Not only does the suspect feel guilty about the original act but also now about having to lie about it. For this person, the decision to confess is still based on the weighing of benefits to consequences. With the less "moral" person, there may be no guilt at all for the original act or the lie.

In either case, the suspect must be made to feel that it is more beneficial to tell the truth than to lie. In the case of the moral suspect, you use third-party hypothetical scenarios to point out that lying is wrong. For example, you might say, "It would be wrong for a person to lie." Keeping the lies to a minimum means fewer obstacles later when having to get this person to admit to the lies in addition to the original act.

The less moral person is not worried about the lie, and the internal dialogue will be more about how he can con his way through the investigation and interrogation. In fact, this suspect may have become so accustomed to lying that he prides himself on his ability to lie, and he may enjoy doing it.

Whether dealing with a moral or less moral suspect, when either one confronts the consequences of their behavior, it will cause a denial. Denial is a way of ignoring or otherwise minimizing the act, whether it is a lie or the original act.

Denials can occur in exaggeration, avoidance, misrepresentation, or other forms. Some eventually confess to overcoming the guilt of the original act; this is an example of catharsis. This alone operates as enough benefit to outweigh the consequence of having to hang on to the guilt. It is important for all individuals to maintain some dignity. The guilty do this by diminishing the seriousness of their actions. Increasing the benefits or decreasing the perceived consequences of the crime or act can also enable one to maintain dignity.

THE INTERROGATOR'S CREDIBILITY

In some cases, a suspect will try to measure your incompetence to determine what kind of denial to make. If you do not appear confident or give the impression that you do not know what you are talking about, the suspect will think he can get around you and thus will continue to make denials.

To prevent this from happening, you must know the facts and be confident in any conclusions you put forth. In addition, you should stay with facts you know and avoid discussing them if possible. The words you choose to express your case can communicate a lack of confidence in the suspect's guilt, for example, "Maybe this happened," or "You could be the one." However, you do not want to express confidence in the suspect's guilt if you cannot establish it. This is a skill you will develop over time. Without confidence, it is suggested that you avoid making any specific remarks about guilt, so you can project confidence without losing credibility.

As will soon become evident, the suspect's belief in your credibility, the credibility of the investigation, and your belief of the suspect's guilt are paramount to getting the suspect past denial.

ACCUSATIONS

Accusation is the stage of the interrogation when you accuse the suspect of committing the act in question. This occurs when you have established with evidence and other interviews or interrogations that the suspect is culpable. Accusation refers to what you say to the suspect, not necessarily other formal methods of legal action. When making an accusation, you must convince the suspect that you are certain of the suspect's guilt. This goes back to the credibility of the investigation and interrogation as well as your demeanor in expressing this confidence. If you exude confidence in your interrogation, you will have fewer denials from the suspect and a greater chance of getting a complete confession.

One strategy you can use when making an accusation is to let the suspect provide his version of the facts surrounding the incident. Then, once the suspect is committed to his story, you confront his lie. The way this strategy works is while the suspect is providing his account of the incident, you express interest and belief, encouraging the suspect to provide as much information as possible. At times, you ask the suspect to give more details. When the suspect is finished, you ask him if he is certain of his story. This locks him in. All the while, based on the facts of the investigation, you already know that the suspect's story is a lie. Later, you confront the suspect with the truth. This gives you great credibility and lets the suspect know that you will not listen to any more denials. This technique works only with factually strong cases.

Direct Accusations

A direct accusation is when you pointedly accuse the suspect of committing an offense or other act grounding liability. Direct accusations are usually limited to cases in which the facts are known and there are few incidences to be addressed. For example, an interrogator would not want to directly accuse a suspect of one burglary when he may be responsible for more than one. In this type of situation, if you accuse the suspect of only one burglary, you have essentially told the suspect that you know about only that one burglary rather than many - the suspect will feel more comfortable in making denials.

A problem with the direct accusation is that it forces the suspect to make a direct denial. This is worse if it is early in the interrogation. Therefore, direct accusations must be used and placed in the interrogation with care.

It is appropriate to make a direct accusation when the suspect makes a denial. When this occurs, you re-accuse the suspect as soon as the denial is made - this is done as a means of maintaining your credibility. You match the way the denial was made. If the suspect uses a soft and easy tone, you re-accuse in the same manner.

Before making a direct accusation, you start with an introduction in which you mention what the investigation is about and what general investigative techniques have been implemented. During the introduction, you are cognizant of deceptive behavior. You must make sure that you communicate the accusation clearly so there is no confusion on the part of the suspect. You can then wait for a response and handle it accordingly. As you re-accuse the suspect in response to his denials, you begin to move to rationalizations. This turns the suspect's attention away from trying to deceive, to thinking about how what he did is not that bad and that it may not be such a terrible thing to admit to.

The direct accusation should always be used with care. It can put the suspect in the position of having to lie. Then later, the suspect will have to admit the lie as well. Unless the purpose is to ruin credibility later (as in the case where the investigation is strong), the direct accusation can cause unnecessary complications.

Indirect Accusations

An indirect accusation involves the same introduction as a direct accusation but approaches the suspect's guilt more indirectly. This is appropriate in cases in which the evidence about the suspect is more circumstantial and when you are not sure that you have all crimes and/or facts regarding the suspect. You discuss investigative techniques, such as video, eyewitnesses, and paper trail evidence. You also hypothetically, and in the third person, mention someone may have committed the act. You do not outwardly indicate that you know the suspect committed the act in a certain way. The purpose is to watch for stressful behavior. If the suspect is innocent, he will listen with interest as you tell him something he has never heard before. The guilty suspect will have an "Oh no, they got me" look. Again, you look for stressful behavior. This technique can help determine who is guilty and who is not. By covering other hypothetical crimes and methods, you can see if the suspect may have been responsible for other crimes (or may be able to expand on crimes he already knows about).

Also of great value during the indirect method is to state why people engage in particular behaviors. You continue to use hypothetical situations like the incident in question without implicating the suspect. As you describes the hypothetical scenarios, you look for stressful behavior on the part of the suspect. By doing this, you will be able to tell what rationalizations to use with the suspect. For example, if discussing theft, you may first mention that some do it for money but others do it for revenge or because it's easy. The suspect's nonverbal responses to the various rationalizations should give you some indication of why he may have done it. Also, by mentioning the "why," you create the impression that you are not judgmental and that you understand the suspect. This increases rapport and increases the likelihood of admission. You can also ask the suspect why he thinks someone would commit the crime. Often, it will be the reason that the suspect used.

Moving Toward Submission

Once you have accused the suspect, directly or indirectly, and the suspect appears to be moving to a point of submission, you can turn the hypothetical situations and third-person accounts to the suspect and situation at hand. You approach any accusations at this point in an understanding yet convincing manner. Once you have established with the suspect that he committed the act, you begin to use development questions that exaggerate what may have been done. For example, the suspect has just nodded his head that he has taken something from the company. Then you might say, "How much? Was it $20,000?" You are using a dollar amount that you know is high, hoping to make the suspect feel that the true dollar amount is not that bad and he will be more likely to admit to the true and whole amount.

Feigning Ignorance

Feigning ignorance refers to suspects who rationalize or deny his behavior by saying he didn't know what he did was wrong. When this occurs, you respond by soliciting as much information from the suspect as you can regarding the violation or event. For example, in a case involving intentional violations of company policy, you might ask the suspect to explain the policy in question prior to any implication of guilt. If the suspect accurately defines or describes the policy, he cannot claim he was unaware of it when confronted with the violation of it.

RATIONALIZATION

Rationalization is the process of offering excuses or justification for the suspect's acts to make it easier to make an admission. The basic idea is to offer a "light at the end of the tunnel," as a diversion from the negative side of the situation to a positive side. You can do this by transferring responsibility to the employer, society, or the "system" if that is appropriate. During rationalization, you do most of the talking, making suggestions as to why the suspect committed the offense. The result is the suspect believes you understand him and care about what happens to him. This will increase rapport.

During rationalization, you remove the suspect's hope that he is not implicated and that the investigation is just going to go away. It is erased when you establish the credibility of the investigation and offer rationalizations as a means of working toward a resolution.

As you begin to suggest rationalizations, you must keep in mind how rationalization may hinder your case. If you offer a rationalization that takes away a mental element of a crime, for example, you may need to go back and correct it if it was originally inaccurate. If you offer the rationalization that the theft was just the suspect "borrowing" the money, when you know it was not, you have removed the "intent to permanently deprive" as the mental element of larceny. After the admission is out, it is easier to bring the suspect around to a full confession - that the suspect had not intended to put the money back.

Consider Motive

When determining what rationalization will be effective, you need to identify the suspect's motive. Finding the right motive involves assessing why the suspect may have committed the act, considering the circumstances of the case and the information in his background. Common motivations include financial need, extravagant spending habits, dislike for the victim, or a drug problem. You can identify the correct motive by observing the suspect's behavior when hypothesizing a motive.

The Right Rationalization

You will know you have chosen the right rationalization when the suspect exhibits an accepting and relieved demeanor. His eyes will open and become more moist and relaxed. His body will relax and his posture will change from a closed posture with crossed arms/legs and body turned away to a more open posture. In addition, denials will decrease in intensity and frequency. If the suspect is not responding to the suggested rationalizations, he will exhibit many of the stressful behaviors discussed earlier. If this is observed, you need to suggest alternative rationalizations. When suggesting rationalization, you use third-person hypothetical scenarios because they are less threatening than first-person scenarios. You may suggest a rationalization that the suspect accepts without having previously thought about it.

One strategy for rationalization is when you compare the suspect's crime or act to something more serious. You make the suspect's incident sound common and day-to-day while casting a more serious tone on more serious crimes. For example, you might say, "Taking something isn't exactly like you're robbing them!" This minimizes the crime or act and allows the suspect to retain some dignity.

Another strategy is you point out that the incident is only one small part of the suspect's life and the other areas of his life are positive and good. By pointing out the good parts of the suspect's past and future, you minimize the incident and making it easier for the suspect to confess.

Additionally, you can tell the suspect that you want his side of the story. You explain that you want the suspect's explanation of the event because the only information you have to that point is what others have reported.

You can also offer rationalizations by mentioning similar cases you have been involved with as a means of showing that the suspect is not alone. This includes contrasting the suspect's case with worse cases, thus minimizing his acts. This can also include discussing a person who is "just like the suspect" such as celebrities, who have been caught drunk driving, taking drugs, or engaged in other crimes. This approach gives an appearance of the humanness of the suspect's actions.

Furthermore, it is helpful if you categorize the suspect's action as a mistake or error in judgment rather than as an intentional act. As a means of casting a positive outlook on the situation, you might tell the suspect how he can learn from his past mistakes. You might say, "The past is the past and there is nothing that can be done to undo it. But the future can be better." You can even suggest motives that show a lack of intent. For example, you might say, "Was this something you thought of on impulse or something you planned out?" The suspect will sooner grab an "impulse" as an answer. Again, be careful not to suggest or say something that may unjustifiably reduce or minimize the elements of the crime or basis of culpability.

In employment cases, rationalizations include blaming the suspect's supervisor or employer for what happened, if appropriate. Inadequate security, low morale, mistreatment, etc., are other common rationalizations if true. You can also blame the system, civil actions, or anything that may have driven the suspect to commit the act. With juveniles, you can blame peer pressure or threats to others. If the suspect uses drugs, you can blame the drugs. Your ability to find and enhance rationalization is based on his creativity and resourcefulness.

Role-Play

Another way of softening a suspect for admission or confession is to role-play. Role-play is when you and suspect decide about a hypothetical person who has committed an act similar to the one the suspect has been accused of committing. Together, you and he decide on appropriate consequences. As the suspect suggests consequences such as termination, probation, or restitution, he begins to accept the idea that he can face the consequences of his actions since he is now doing the judging. Also, as you discuss hypothetical scenarios, you guide the suspect to the idea that investigations are not witch hunts. You establish that the investigation is not a personal attack on the suspect; it is a humane and understanding process. This strategy touches on the fear the suspect has in admitting to the offense. Role-playing is used in limited circumstances because it focuses on the consequences of actions and can backfire. Also, you need to be careful about implied promises, for example, implications that legal consequences will be lessened if the suspect confesses.

THE ADMISSION OR CONFESSION

In Chapter 1, admission was defined as a statement from which guilt may be inferred, but is short of a confession. A confession was defined as a voluntary statement acknowledging guilt. These definitions are frequently used interchangeably, however, they have different meanings. An interrogator may obtain only an admission inferring guilt from his suspect. Sometimes full confessions are difficult to obtain.

By the time the suspect is ready to confess, he has been through a very emotional situation and is exhausted. He has stopped fighting the benefit/consequence argument in his mind, has accepted what he has done, and realizes he must admit his actions. When this occurs, specific body language will be evident. The suspect will begin to withdraw. Eye contact will be minimal and he may look down and to the left as he thinks internally. His head may drop and his body may slump forward.

During this phase, you increase the frequency with which you mention general rationalizations with limited detail. This helps shift the mood of the interrogation into admission. You begin to move closer to the suspect while maintaining a conversation. This is to maintain contact with the suspect, who may be so withdrawn he may hear very little you say. You want to maintain the suspect's attention, so he does not change emotional states and revert back to denial.

Not all suspects exhibit this withdrawn look. However, generally, there is a shift in behavior when the suspect is ready to begin admitting guilt. The suspect may become calm, perhaps even excited as he decides to end the frustration. Whatever the case, determining whether the suspect is ready to make an admission can be a difficult task. You do not want to move too soon because the suspect may deny guilt. If the moment is right, you should take the opportunity without delay.

When you sense the suspect is ready to make an admission, you use soft accusation questions. Soft accusation questions are leading in nature and show your resolve in the suspect's guilt. For example, rather than saying, "Did you take the money?" You would say, "How much money did you take?" This does not leave room for a denial.

Widen the Scope of the Admission

During the admission stage of the interrogation, you ask broad-based questions. You do not want to ask questions that are too narrow because you may not know the sum of the suspect's crimes. To illustrate, if you ask, "How many thefts from the company have you been responsible for?", it may limit the response. The suspect may respond with "one." A better approach would be to ask, "How many times have you done similar things policy in the recent past?" He may respond with acts you knew nothing about. Also, you do not limit the frequency of violations or the scope of the violations. Most suspects have done much more than you are aware of and they have usually broken more than one law.

DENIAL REVISITED

If a suspect begins to regress and make a denial, you stop the denial and re-accuse the suspect in the same manner as the denial was made. If the denial is made in an assertive manner, you re-accuse in an assertive manner. If the denial was slow and soft, you re-accuse that way. Then you return to rationalization. If the suspect stops and pauses after a question, he might be ready to make an admission. You should be ready by offering an exaggeration, for example, "Did you steal $100,000?" The suspect may say, "No way, it was only $10,000."

THE FIRST ADMISSION

The first admission is the hardest to get but will make the others easier. The first one is usually only partially true; the suspect provides a piece of the truth in the hopes that you will buy it. When this occurs, you continue with rationalization and follow up with more specific questions as a means of opening and developing the admission. For example, "Did you take the money to pay for bills?" assumes a theft and asks for a more specific account of what occurred. You can make the questions invited to answer, "Did you take the money to pay for bills or drugs?" In fact, the money may have been taken for drugs, but the suggestion (for bills) makes it easier to admit, even though it is not completely accurate.

You would rather accept a lie as the rationalization and avoid the drug issue to get closer to the suspect making an admission. You can correct the purpose of the theft after the suspect opens up more and becomes more comfortable discussing the entire situation.

Questions and Answers

When asking questions during the admission, it is most effective if you ask in a way that is easy to answer, such as 'yes' or 'no'. The suspect may be withdrawn and not capable of long-involved answers. When an admission occurs, you always acknowledge the admission or confession to establish that you heard it and accepted it. This serves to lessen the suspect's belief that further denials will work. It also rewards the suspect for admitting or confessing to the crime or act and for heading in the "right" direction.

Admission vs. Denial

A suspect's body language will generally indicate if he is going to make an admission or denial. A denial will be more spontaneous. The suspect's head will begin to nod before "no" is spoken. He may begin to inhale, his lips may tighten, and he may make eye contact. You should cut him off before he gets his denial out by turning your head, putting your hand up, and then re-accusing and moving to rationalization. The suspect who is ready to admit will not take the breath as with the denial and will continue to "space out." He will not maintain eye contact. You should recognize this as a possible opportunity to obtain admission.

Confirming You Have the Right Person

If the suspect makes an admission, you continue to explore the details and confirm them as you proceed in the interrogation to confirm that the suspect is the right person. As you obtain more details, you further establish you have the right person because only the person who committed the crime will know where the murder weapon is or how stolen money was spent.

Note Taking

During the initial phases of the admission, it is recommended that you refrain from taking notes. It distracts the suspect and makes him feel that you are taking notes to use against him later. As the admission progresses and the suspect becomes more comfortable, you can take notes and explain to the suspect that you are taking notes so that you do not forget anything. Notes are important to establish where the investigation will proceed.

Using Exaggeration

You can use exaggeration to obtain an admission. When rationalizing and exaggerating, you tell the suspect that you understand that it may be difficult to remember everything. This is especially true in theft situations. The suspect may have taken more than he realizes. It is surprising how it can add up over time. In some cases, theft suspects have admitted to taking only $5 to $10 a week, perhaps only trivial things like sodas or snacks. When added up over a few years, you can easily approach $1,000. This often shocks most suspects.

A good way to develop an admission in a theft case is to start by asking the suspect about the first time he committed a crime, perhaps exaggerating the earliest time it may have happened - for example, "Your first day on the job?" This gives you a window of time within which to develop an average. In this example, you would next ask the suspect how much he took in any given shift. Whatever amount he responds with, you assume the total amount is a lot more. The suspect may reply, "I didn't take money every shift!" After this type of response, you move up to the next time frame, for example, how much he took in an average week, and so on. At some point, you ask, "What's the most that was taken on any one occasion?" The answer to this question establishes another potential boundary. Next, you ask how much on average the suspect took. If the suspect does not give a truthful response, you might respond with, "That does not match what our investigation shows." Hopefully, this will bring the suspect around. Obviously, this technique can be used with other types of crimes as well.

You want to give the impression that you already know what the suspect is telling you. The purpose of asking the questions is to gauge how honest the suspect is; the more he tells you what you already knows, the more honest he is being. It shows cooperation. You can give the suspect a hypothetical:

"Imagine that you have a video showing a person taking $100 from the cash register. You sit the person down and he denies it. After a second question, the person says he took $5. This is a person you know is not being cooperative and who will be difficult to work with. This only compounds the problem. Not only has the person taken something, he isn't being truthful. Those that tell the truth are signaling their desire to make up for their error and that they are not really dishonest."

Once you have a total dollar amount, try to further establish what items were taken, where they may currently be located, etc. For the theft of money, try to establish what the money was spent on. These additional facts help cement the fact that the suspect is guilty and may help with restitution. Look for other areas of theft such as credit card fraud, check forgery, merchandise theft, etc. Again, appear to know the answers. Allude to the fact that the investigation has been thorough and complete and has established many things. Always tell the suspect that he may tell something unknown, but this will just be further proof that he is being honest. Also, tell him that taking $100 is the same as $1... theft is theft. This helps reduce inhibition about expanding on other theft activity. It is a sign that the suspect is truly cooperating and willing to make up for what he has done.

As you develop other areas, you must revisit areas already covered. This will often jog the memory of the suspect and new crimes or acts may come out. This also helps reaffirm that the information you already have is true and accurate. The suspect would likely recant if it were not true. Ask these questions in an assumptive way, "What else did you think of here?" You must be patient if memory does not serve them initially. This is something you want patience with. You can suggest possible items taken as a means of jogging memory. Try to use plurals in the question, "Could you have taken some televisions?" Think of the area where the suspect works or what types of things he has taken in the past (e.g. jewelry, electronics items).

When finished, ask the suspect if there is anything else he feels he should discuss. Mention that the investigation will continue, and you do not want to find out about something that he would have expected the suspect to bring up.

PARTIAL CONFESSIONS OR ADMISSIONS

Partial confession refers to a suspect who tries to negotiate a confession. The suspect may claim to be innocent but still try to bargain with you, for example, the suspect who files a complaint against you (or threatens to) and then offers to drop the complaint if you will leave him alone. Another type of partial confession is the suspect who offers to pay you back for a theft saying he did not do it, but he just wants to get it over with. This is a sign of a guilty person.

Partial confessions also include indirect statements, for example, "I will confess if it will make you happy," or "If someone saw me do it, that must mean I did it." When this occurs, the suspect is trying to say he did it without having to say so directly. you should not respond to these statements. You should let the suspect make the statement and not answer. Answering is encouraging the suspect not to confess completely.

In cases like these, care should be taken not to attempt to obtain an admission or a confession unless it appears likely that the suspect is ready.

Probing Motivations

It can help to ask the suspect to pretend he is the perpetrator and ask what may have motivated him. Any answers he gives may be his true motivation. Facts or methods of committing the crime that were previously unknown may leak out in the process. If this happens, you should begin to transition into an accusation for example, "Isn't this the real reason that you did it...?" You must feel very strongly about the suspect's desire to confess and his readiness when making an accusation.

Another technique you might use is to ask the suspect what mistakes the suspect made in the case being investigated. This will give you insight into the suspect's ability to think like a criminal. People who do not think of or commit crimes will not be able to find flaws in the way the crime was committed. This technique is effective in selective interviews. If a person being interviewed can come up with elaborate answers to your questions, he may be a suspect or may have committed other crimes.

Reaching Out

When a suspect is ready to make a partial admission, he will begin to make statements or inquiries about the potential punishment for the crime. The suspect will usually do this by referring to a hypothetical situation, for example, "What usually happens to people who do this?" You should respond with general possibilities or say that you do not know. The suspect may also ask if the discussion is confidential. This signals that he is entering an acceptance phase and is facing the fact that he can no longer try to deceive. If the suspect appears ready, you stop talking and begin to listen while maintaining a sympathetic and supportive atmosphere. You must not get too zealous about obtaining admission.

THE UNCOOPERATIVE SUSPECT

If the suspect continues to be uncooperative and you do not think he is going to change, you should start the written statement so you have a written record of the information you have obtained to that point in time. You should not reveal any evidence until it is necessary. It may become necessary with a suspect who flatly refuses to admit any involvement. In this type of situation, you can reveal one piece of evidence at a time to refute the suspect's denial. This is can be effective in turning the uncooperative suspect around.

THE WRITTEN STATEMENT

The written statement is a statement written by the suspect detailing his version of the events related to the crime. The purpose of the written statement is to solidify what the suspect has admitted or confessed. It deters the suspect for later changing his story. It can also serve as evidence if the suspect cannot make it to trial (e.g. illness or death) or if the suspect needs to refresh his memory about what he admitted.

The written statement should include only relevant facts and important issues, such as the elements of the crime. If the suspect has admitted to more than one crime, you may need to get separate statements for each one in the event one is inadmissible due to a legal deficiency.

Basic Issues

The written statement is written by the suspect and should address all pieces of evidence. It should begin with biographical information, which gets the suspect into a writing mood, then move into a blanket overall admission. Having the admission at the beginning is helpful if at some point the suspect decides he does not want to continue. Later in the statement, the suspect substantiates the overall admission with the 'who', 'what', 'when', 'where', 'why', and 'how' of each act or crime. You should number the pages to show no page was removed and have the suspect initial on each page to show that nothing was added.

As the suspect completes each page, you remove it from the room. This way, if the suspect becomes reluctant to continue, you will still have the completed pages. Plus, some suspects have been known to tear up the statement. If this were to happen, you would retrieve the torn pages to be used later as evidence.

Types of Written Statements

There are two forms of written statements: narrative and question and answer. The straight narrative is a first-person account of the event and addresses all relevant facts freely and completely. The question-and-answer form consists of very specific answers to specific questions. These can be used as follows up to the narrative to clarify vague items and to help establish important issues. The question-and-answer form is also used when the suspect is too upset to write a long narrative.

Interrogator's Role in Written Statement

It is important that the suspect understands the purpose of the written statement and that he is not coerced into writing the statement. When transitioning into the written statement phase of the interrogation, you ask the suspect to write down his explanation of what happened. It is his side of the story. The statement must be written of the suspect's own free will so he does not later claim he was coerced or he did not write it.

Some suspects will write the written statement but later claim they were coerced into making the statement. To avoid this problem, you keep a written record of requests made by the suspect during the written statement and if they were honored. Examples are trips to the restroom and requests for water. This will dispel suggestion of coercion. Another possibility is to have a witness present during the writing of the statement. If there is a witness, you can read the statement to the suspect in front of the witness and have the suspect acknowledge that it was made of his own free will. Furthermore, you can have the suspect indicate how he feels about making the written statement in some part of the statement. Suspects will often mention that they are happy to cooperate and feel this is a way they can help undo what was done. It is also recommended that you have the suspect indicated in the opening parts of the written statement that the suspect was not coerced or promised anything in return for the statement. These procedures will make a claim of coercion difficult to sustain.

Another problem that occurs with a written statement is the suspect may later claim he did not make the statement. If this transpires, you can point out misspellings, slang, or unique handwriting that the suspect used when writing the statement. To prevent this from occurring, you have the suspect initial any changes that were made during the writing of the statement to show that the suspect was aware they were made.

At times, a suspect will be unable to write a statement due to language barriers or illiteracy, and or will refuse to give one. If the suspect cannot speak the language, a translator can be used for the written statement. In this situation, a witness is required to listen to the oral admission. The witness then writes a written statement documenting the oral admission. This could also be used with a witness who refuses to write a written statement.

Some Methods to Determine Honesty in the Written Statement

There are several methods you can use to determine honesty in the written statement. One is where the suspect writes the statement on a hard writing surface and with a hard writing implement, such as a ballpoint pen. Here, the writing will be evident at the back of the statement.

This can reveal a clue; areas, where the writing has been harder and pierced through the paper, are sections where the suspect was writing about stressful events. The reason the writing is harder is that the body releases adrenaline, and thus the muscles become more rigid and less coordinated. The writing will reflect this. Stalling behavior can also be noted by changes in the suspect's handwriting. Also, subsequent writings will generally have less information in them and will be more cursory as the suspect sees his culpability in writing again.

Written Report about the Written Statement

In addition to the statement, prepare a written report of the investigation as well as detailing what was said in the interrogation. This should include the interrogation notes if possible.

ENDING THE INTERROGATION

You end the interrogation in a professional and courteous manner. If it did not result in a confession or admission, you do not become upset; not all suspects will confess and some of the more street-wise suspects will never confess. Some may even taunt you purposely. You leave the option open to an interview or interrogation again. If the suspect refuses to confess, you allow the suspect to speak and move on to less important topics as a means of changing the subject and taking the negative edge off the unsuccessful atmosphere. This may include discussing other crimes or inquiring about other possible suspects. By allowing the suspect to talk and discuss other areas, you give the suspect the chance to vent and release the tension of being accused. The interrogation ends with you explaining why the interrogation was conducted and why the suspect was implicated (without giving away any sensitive information). You do not apologize for having to make the accusation. Instead, the subject focuses on the facts and logic of the investigation. You thank the suspect for his time and cooperation and leave the door open for future contact.

CONCLUSION

Each interview or interrogation is a learning experience. By applying the techniques, theories, and responses covered in this book, the novice interrogator will a new world of interview and interrogation. You can enhance your existing style or develop a style of operating that is effective, suits your personality, and achieve the ultimate result: The Truth!

SUMMARY

An effective interrogator controls the interrogation by asking a variety of types of questions designed to elicit specific information. You must be cognizant of verbal and non-verbal signs of deception, denial, and acceptance and be prepared to address these issues. Furthermore, skilled interrogators use rationalizations to obtain admissions or confessions when appropriate. Interrogations always conclude with a written statement signed by the suspect.

DISCUSSION QUESTIONS

- What does "determine a baseline" mean? What types of questions would you ask when determining a baseline?
- What innate human response are most signs of deception based upon? Describe this human response.
- What is denial and when does it generally occur?
- Define acceptance.
- When is it appropriate to make an accusation?
- Why would an interrogator offer rationalizations to a suspect?
- What is the purpose of the written statement?

PART 2.

EYEWITNESS EVIDENCE

STOP

CHAPTER 7.

EYEWITNESS EVIDENCE: AN INTRODUCTION

CHAPTER OVERVIEW

Eyewitnesses are an important part of an investigation. Generally, when an investigator interviews an eyewitness, he walks the witness through the event, asks a few probing questions for clarification, and then writes a report. However, there are many issues related to eyewitness evidence that can affect the case. Prior to using eyewitness evidence, investigators need to be familiar with the research conducted by psychologists and lawyers involving eyewitness evidence.

OBJECTIVE

To teach the reader how to define eyewitness evidence.

INTRODUCTION

Imagine an interrogator is in a courtroom, on the stand. An attorney, on cross-examination, is reading aloud his report for the jury and judge to hear. The report contains the interrogator's interview with an eyewitness. The attorney reads his interview as follows:

The interrogator: "Tell me what happened."

Witness: "I had just turned out the lights and was going to bed. A few minutes later, I saw a man with a green shirt jump through my bedroom window. He pointed a gun at me and took the money from my desk. He then ran out the same window."

The interrogator: "How long did you view this man?"

Witness: "It must have been at least 5 minutes."

The interrogator: "Did you see the hat he was wearing?"

Witness: "Ah... yes, I saw a hat."

The interrogator: "Are you sure about that?" Witness: "Yes."

The interrogator: "Absolutely certain?"

Witness: "Yes."

The attorney then turns to the interrogator and says,

Attorney: "Are you aware of the term 'dark adaptation'?"

The interrogator: "Ah... no."

Attorney: "You wrote that the witness saw the shirt as green and had just turned the lights out. Did you know that it takes the human eye about 5 minutes to adapt to darkness and, further, that color vision in the dark is rarely very good?"

The interrogator: "Ah... no."

Attorney: "You wrote in your report that the witness saw the subject for 5 minutes. Did you know that research has shown that people tend to overestimate the duration of an event, especially when they are stressed?"

The interrogator: "Ah... no."

Attorney: "Are you aware of a term called 'weapon focus'?"

The interrogator: "Ah... no."

Attorney: "You wrote that the subject stuck a gun in her face. Are you aware that weapon focus causes the victim to focus more on the gun instead of on the other features of the subject?"

The interrogator: "Ah... no."

Attorney: "Are you aware that this witness takes diazepam, a prescription drug, to calm her nerves?"

The interrogator: "No."

Attorney: "Are you aware that there is research that shows that diazepam causes a drop in eyewitness accuracy?"

The interrogator: "No,"

Attorney: "You asked the witness if she had seen, and I quote, 'the' hat. You then asked her two times if she was sure. Did you know there is research that shows that even such subtle question wording as 'the' hat as opposed to saying 'a' hat can cause the witness to adopt into memory a hat where there was no such earlier recognition? Did you also know that repetition of that statement can further increase the witness's adoption of your suggestive statement into memory?"

The interrogator: "Aaaah... no."

Attorney: "Is it your position that this witness saw my client's face for 5 minutes, that she saw a green shirt and a hat?"

The interrogator: "I'm not sure."

Attorney: "Are you aware that these are the only things that link my client to the crime?"

The interrogator: "I guess."

Attorney: "You're not sure and you guess."

You get the picture. While this is entirely fictitious (and arguably not realistic), this scenario points out the embarrassment you could be put through. It can be seen why it would have helped to know these things ahead of the interview of the eyewitness. You could have pointed out the unreliability of the statement before it was submitted to evidence. You could also have saved yourself embarrassment by knowing what questions to ask and how to ask them.

Many times, the eyewitness is merely a part of the overall investigation. You are told about an event that you need to investigate. You know there is a witness you needs to talk to and you go to talk to that person. You walk the witness through the event, asks a few probing questions to clarify, and then go home to dinner.

However, most investigators do not realize how much impact they can have on that interview. It is known that you should not "lead" the witness and not to put words into the witness's mouth, but there are other intricacies that exist that might help or hurt the accuracy of the information obtained from that interview. The investigator will find that there are many issues that can have a devastating or, conversely, a positive impact on what he is providing as fact from that witness.

Many parts of this part of the book are fascinating and intriguing. Each phase of the investigation, the psychological issues and legal issues that can help or hinder the investigation will be discussed. It is commonly known that facts from an eyewitness interview can determine guilt or innocence. The importance cannot be stressed enough!

A NOTE ABOUT THIS PART OF THE BOOK

As will be seen, the psychological and legal issues brought up can be very involved, requiring years of schooling and experience. Most of the research covered herein was performed by psychologists with advanced degrees, many of whom devote much of their lives to this very subject. It would be difficult for one book to cover all issues to the depth that would be required for a working knowledge of a given area of discipline. Also, legal implications are not simple. Many attorneys have devoted many years to understanding and creating the legal doctrine that shapes this area. Again, one book cannot adequately cover all areas to the extent necessary.

The scope and purpose, then, is to give the interviewer an overall flavor of what goes on in the area of eyewitness evidence, as it might concern the investigator. Any actual training, interpretation, or research should always be done by a trained professional in that given area (e.g. a psychologist or attorney). The interviewer may wish to consult a supervisor, attorney, or psychologist for specifics on how the investigation might be helped or hindered by the issues contained in this book. Additionally, much of the research and existing beliefs about the subject of eyewitness evidence point to its unreliability. It might appear that this would favor the defense rather than the prosecution. That is, it is usually the prosecution/plaintiff or plaintiff who puts forth an eyewitness to support a claim. It is not the intention of this book to favor either side. Both the defense and the prosecution will, at some point, need to put forward an eyewitness. Each side will need to understand how the issues in eyewitness evidence might lead to the truth or an erroneous conclusion. The purpose is to increase the truth-gathering process and to educate all concerned to this end.

SUMMARY

Eyewitness evidence is an important component of the investigation. However, for eyewitness evidence to be effective, the investigator must be familiar with the research conducted by lawyers and psychologists regarding eyewitness evidence.

CHAPTER 8.

EYEWITNESS EVIDENCE

CHAPTER OVERVIEW

Eyewitness evidence is an important part of an investigation because it is direct evidence. However, it can also lead to erroneous conclusions when the eyewitness is wrong. Research demonstrates that the perception of the general public is if an eyewitness said it happened, then it did. Eyewitness evidence is potentially unpredictable and inaccurate.

OBJECTIVES

To teach the reader how to...

- Identify why eyewitness evidence is important to an investigation.
- Identify inherent problems with eyewitness evidence.

Since the first printing of this book, significant and important developments have occurred in the area of the interview of the eyewitness. These developments denote a coming together of experts in this area, e.g. psychologists, attorneys, and investigators.

Laws vary by jurisdiction and there may be ongoing changes in the recommended guidelines and procedures that should be used when dealing with eyewitness evidence. It cannot be stressed enough how important it is to check with the interviewer's agency/department policy, the local district attorney, or other appropriate professional for the proper guidelines and procedures when dealing with eyewitness evidence. Anything presented in this book should be reviewed and interpreted consistent with those guidelines and procedures; they will take precedence.

The second thing to consider is the more knowledge you has, the better able you are to know what information and evidence to obtain. Often, the investigator has the first and only contact with the witness prior to court. How did the witness feel during the event? Was he or she doing anything while the event occurred? Has the witness seen the defendant before or since? Has the witness been questioned by anyone else and what was asked and answered? As this book progresses, these are all important questions to be considered. Generally, the earlier you are in the process, the better the evidence will be when it is obtained.

Finally, it is possible to hurt the case without knowledge of certain issues concerning the interview. It is important to know that question wording, repetition of questioning, the interrogator's demeanor, etc., are issues important to understand (all covered later).

The ensuing information is important not only to help the client but also to help the interviewer understand what is important and unimportant evidence. It also helps him keep his own efforts from becoming the problem rather than the solution.

IMPORTANCE OF EYEWITNESS EVIDENCE IN GENERAL

First, eyewitness evidence plays an important role in the legal system. Eyewitness evidence is direct evidence, the best kind there is, as opposed to indirect or circumstantial evidence. And to many, eyewitness evidence is the best kind of direct evidence. One 1976 study done in England reviewed 2,116 lineups and found that in 45% of these lineups, a defendant was identified. Of the 850 of these that were prosecuted, 82% were convicted. In 347 of these cases, the only evidence was one or more eyewitnesses, yet 74% of them resulted in a conviction. It is easy to see that an eyewitness plays a major role in the outcome of a case.

Second, society puts a lot of confidence in the eyewitness. But should they? There are many misconceptions about eyewitness evidence, one of which is the accuracy of the eyewitness. As will be seen below, the issues here are not insignificant.

EYEWITNESS EVIDENCE THAT IS WRONG

Nothing is more poorly understood in the human body than the brain. Unfortunately, many aspects of eyewitness evidence are based here. Though the knowledge of the brain and how it works increases daily, there does not exist the level of exactness necessary to satisfy the legal system. Individuals want proof that a subject is guilty or innocent, responsible or not. However, when one tries to extract information from the witness, they cannot always be sure if they are getting accurate information or nonsense. It is this unpredictability of the brain versus the demand for perfect accuracy that has created many of the issues that will come up as these topics are explored.

In 1975, a study was conducted wherein a television station showed a 12-second mock robbery. Of the 2000 people that called in, only 14% correctly chose the defendant out of a photo lineup of 6 people (note that this is nearly the same percentage one would get by just guessing!).

In another study conducted in 1932, 65 cases were reviewed where an innocent person had been convicted. The major cause of this was the improper identification of the defendant where a violent crime was involved. This mistake was the case for 29 of the 65 (almost one-third!). In 8, the wrongly accused looked nothing like the actual perpetrator and in 12 it was not close (according to the study).

The fact is eyewitnesses can lead to erroneous conclusions in many cases. In one paper, it was suggested that the rate of wrongful conviction, based largely on problems with eyewitness identification, in the United States could be as high as 5%. Even more conservative estimates of 0.6% might lead to the wrongful conviction of 10,000 or more people per year. Not insignificant numbers!

MISCONCEPTIONS ABOUT EYEWITNESS EVIDENCE

At times, individuals have more confidence in the witness than they should. In an experiment conducted in 1974, subjects were asked to play the role of jurors. They were given a scenario in which the evidence for both the defense and the prosecution was even, yet only 18% of the 50 jurors voted for conviction. Then another series of jurors was given the same scenario, but they were told that the store clerk (for a mock robbery) had "seen" the shooting; the rest of the evidence was otherwise the same. The second set of jurors voted 72% to convict. In yet a third series of jurors, an additional fact was added: the clerk's eyewitness had extremely poor vision. Yet 68% were convicted - even with poor vision. It is easy to see from the research the perception of lay people is that if an eyewitness says it happened, they are more likely to believe it did.

Another common misconception regarding eyewitness evidence is that ordinary citizens believe people remember more about violent events than non-violent events. This is simply not true. People are just as likely to overestimate an event as they are to underestimate an event, regardless of the degree of violence.

RECENT DEVELOPMENTS

With the advent of DNA evidence in recent years, it has been possible to prove innocence or guilt with greater certainty. As such, it is now possible to examine errors that have led to erroneous or wrongful convictions.

The National Institute of Justice Research Report, Convicted by Juries, Case Studies in the Use of DNA Evidence to Establish Innocence After Trial, reviewed 28 convictions that were proved to be wrongful due to the introduction of new DNA evidence, i.e. proved that there was defendant innocent. The most compelling evidence in most of these wrongful convictions was eyewitness evidence. This is what prompted the (then) Attorney General Janet Reno to create the Technical Working Group on Eyewitness Evidence in 1998. In forming this group, it was her purpose to attempt to establish why eyewitness evidence could have led to so many wrongful convictions and to see if the professional community in this area could come up with, and agree upon, possible solutions.

CONCLUSION

This area is central to the legal system and the investigator. In addition, people on the street who are potential jurors, prosecutors, judges, etc., generally believe that an eyewitness account is going to be accurate. Eyewitness evidence is potentially unpredictable and inaccurate. The legal process and the people in it may be sending the wrong person to jail, setting the wrong person free, or holding others accountable for something that they did not do.

SUMMARY

Eyewitness evidence is an important component of the investigation because it is direct evidence. However, eyewitness evidence is inherently unpredictable due to errors made by eyewitnesses. Research shows that eyewitness evidence is very powerful although often inaccurate.

DISCUSSION QUESTIONS

- What kind of evidence is eyewitness evidence?
- Why is eyewitness evidence important to an investigator?
- Is eyewitness evidence reliable? Why or why not?

CHAPTER 9.

THE INTERVIEWER'S IMPACT ON THE LEGAL SYSTEM

CHAPTER OVERVIEW

Eyewitness evidence is a central part of the legal process. Misconceptions about eyewitness evidence can lead to a miscarriage of justice. It is important for the investigator to understand each stage of the legal process and how his actions can affect the process. There are many things that can affect specific areas of the legal system. This chapter covers some of the issues, from admissibility to direct examination of the witness, to cross-examination, then to closing arguments, and finally the burden of proof.

OBJECTIVES

To teach the reader how to...

- Define the pretrial terms discovery, motion, admissibility, and expert testimony.
- Define the trial terms direct examination, cross-examination, closing argument, and burden of proof.

BEFORE TRIAL

Discovery

The first issue is discovery, which is the process that the legal community uses to gather and enhance evidence prior to trial. Often, it will be used to determine

the strengths and weaknesses of each case. However, this process is very expensive. Rather than waiting for discovery, a comprehensive preliminary investigation may answer questions that other investigators and attorneys might wait for the discovery process to answer. This saves time and money and may lead to an earlier determination of whether to go to trial or to settle (depending on the strength of the case). Of course, this may not necessarily remove the need for discovery but might lessen the need for much of it.

Often, too, the tactical approach of the discovery can be determined by what is uncovered in the interview. A deposition (where witnesses are interviewed under oath) might give away information one does not want the opposition to know about. Avoiding discovery altogether might be desirable if a proper interview is given as the reason.

The bottom line here is the attorney and investigator who know the intricacies of what can influence an eyewitness are in a better position to know what will be at issue in discovery. Such targets are commonly the witness's perception, witness memory, and witness recall, as will be discussed in later chapters.

Motions Prior to Trial

A motion is a legal maneuver wherein an attorney submits a document to the court that seeks to have the court rule in his favor. Often legal authority, backed with factual data, will be included. Psychological findings and research papers for eyewitness evidence can be included in these motions. An attorney cannot know to include them if they do not know they exist or if they could become an issue. It is often best to cite the problem and then have a psychologist and/or attorney determine the application to the case. Issues of suggestibility, the violence of the event, and others might be raised, and then cited accordingly.

Admissibility

To be admitted into evidence for court, evidence must be both probative and material. Probative means that it tends to logically prove what it is offered for, and material means that it is of some consequence to the case. The interviewer's knowledge of this can help establish how a statement can be viewed to be more likely to be admitted.

Conversely, admission of a statement will be suppressed or denied admission into evidence if it is "made under circumstances which were so unnecessarily suggestive as to give rise to a very substantial likelihood of irreparable misidentification". This is usually determined by a totality of the circumstances, that is, there is no clear rule as to when something is unnecessarily suggestive or not. Even if something was obtained from an eyewitness in a suggestive manner, it can still be admitted if it appears to be overall reliable. What does this mean? Basically, if something is not reliable, it can be suppressed. The importance here is obvious. If your interview, or something else that you do, manages to cross this line, it won't be admitted. As important, however, is your ability to establish that a statement is reliable or that the opponent's is not.

So how do you establish reliability? A major court case cited some factors such as the ability to see the offender, frequency, and duration of viewing, lighting, violence or stress of an event, cultural expectations, degree of certainty, the degree of attention of the witness during the crime, and the overall complexity of events, etc. The entire list of possibilities is very long and beyond the scope of this book. Nonetheless, some help and some hurt. Many of the issues covered later in this book can help to establish reliability or unreliability. It becomes, at some point, a matter of common sense. As mentioned before, trained psychologists and/or attorneys can help establish this for court.

Your understanding of these issues can help you establish the logical, material, and reliable aspects of evidence and what they need to do to make it so.

Expert Testimony

Expert testimony is not particularly relevant to the investigator. However, it is placed here to establish the role the investigator can play in helping to establish the need for an expert. Often, a court will not allow testimony by anyone about the psychological factors that can impact an eyewitness account. This is especially the case where there are no specific factors in the case that would call up a need for it. Merely calling an expert witness, a trained psychologist in this area, to educate the jury on the general issues will not be enough. The court often requires the expert witness to testify only to factors that are found to be of consequence in the specific case.

This is where the investigator comes in. By identifying possible issues and, more importantly, by being able to expand on them during the investigation and interview, counsel will have something to get the expert on the stand. Getting this expert on the stand is of great importance to legal counsel. In fact, in some cases, the denial of an expert can be considered a denial of due process of law and can become malpractice for the attorney if the subject does not seek one. The expert input can make or break the case, especially if the eyewitness is the only or the most important evidence.

AT TRIAL

Direct Examination

On direct examination, the eyewitness is usually asked to recount what occurred. A witness will be more believable to a jury if the witness is more credible. Clear, accurate, and detailed testimony will give the witness an increased perception of credibility. A recent study proved that jurors would find a witness more persuasive who provides more detail than one who does not. This may be due in part to the belief by the jurors that the witness has a better memory and that the witness paid closer attention to the event. Therefore, it is important to get as detailed a recounting of the event from the witness as possible.

Frequently, direct examination will follow the flow of the interview. The interview frequently follows the chronology of the event. Jurors and eyewitnesses seem to prefer this chronology, as it is easy to follow and easy to work around. This can be the preferred flow in the interviews. Other issues can come into play here (see the Interview section of this book).

Cross-Examination

Cross-examination is used to test the credibility of the witness after direct examination. It is usually limited to things brought up on direct examination and the type of questioning that is allowed is more liberal. For example, leading questions (those that suggest an answer) are allowed on cross-examination but not usually on a direct exam. Attorneys will usually use cross-examination to discredit the eyewitness, often in the area of witness memory, witness perception, and witness ability to recall. The attorney questioning the witness will look for witness omissions or witness contradictions in prior statements. If, during the interview, the witness did not indicate the color of the defendant's automobile in a crash, the fact that the witness later recalled the color leaves the cross-examining attorney with the proposition to the jury that the color was never actually seen in the first place. This is another reason to be sure that one gets as much specific information from the witness during the interview as possible, without pressuring a response or suggesting one (of course).

Many times, it is a good idea to obtain the other (opposing) investigator's file if it is legally available. If that investigator has already interviewed the witness, his interview may contain information that could be valuable to discredit the witness. This assumes that the witness is injurious to the case. Did the investigator properly question the witness? Are there any major gaps in the factual statements, e.g. the color of the car as above? Does anything about the statement provided by the witness contradict other factual findings? Attorneys look for anything they could potentially use on cross-examination.

Closing Arguments

Closing arguments are what an attorney will give to the jury, or judge in a trial by judge, at the close of the trial. They summarize and accentuate that side's case, and this topic is beyond the primary scope of this book. However, closing arguments can be the most important part of the case. It is the last thing the jury or judge hears. Closing arguments are a compilation of what has been available up to that point. As such, all the previously mentioned aspects of the legal process become more significant. Often, it will have more impact if specifics are given rather than a flood of generic words. The investigator's ability to find and enhance specific issues applied to specific facts in a case will help here. This allows the attorney to properly prepare what can successfully be said and what should be avoided or explained away.

BURDEN OF PROOF

Also, important to know is the definition of "burden of proof". The burden of proof determines who has the burden to prove the specific legal theory and to what level. For example, in criminal cases, the prosecution has the burden of proving each allegation beyond a reasonable doubt. Regardless of who has the burden of proof (and the corresponding level to which it must be met), knowing the burden of proof can make an investigator's job more, or less, difficult.

CONCLUSION

In conclusion, each stage of the legal process is impacted by what investigators do, and those actions can help and/or hurt. By understanding the importance of the investigator's role in this legal process, one is better equipped to know why it is important to have at least some knowledge of the issues that will follow in this book and which can be found elsewhere. Additionally, it is safer to save actual interpretation and implementation for the attorneys and/or psychologists.

Eyewitness evidence is a central part of the legal process and of human's lives in general. Misconceptions about this subject can lead to holding the wrong person accountable and letting those responsible go without facing justice. This chapter has helped to point out why it is important to understand the basic legal issues involved in this subject. It is possible to find other areas of inquiry and significance.

SUMMARY

It is important for the investigator to understand the legal process and his role within it. Eyewitness evidence is a central part of this process, and misconceptions regarding eyewitness evidence can lead to wrongful convictions.

DISCUSSION QUESTIONS

- Why should an investigator be knowledgeable about the components of the legal process?
- Briefly explain the four components of pre-trial preparation as it concerns eyewitness evidence and the investigator.
- What is the difference between direct examination and cross-examination?

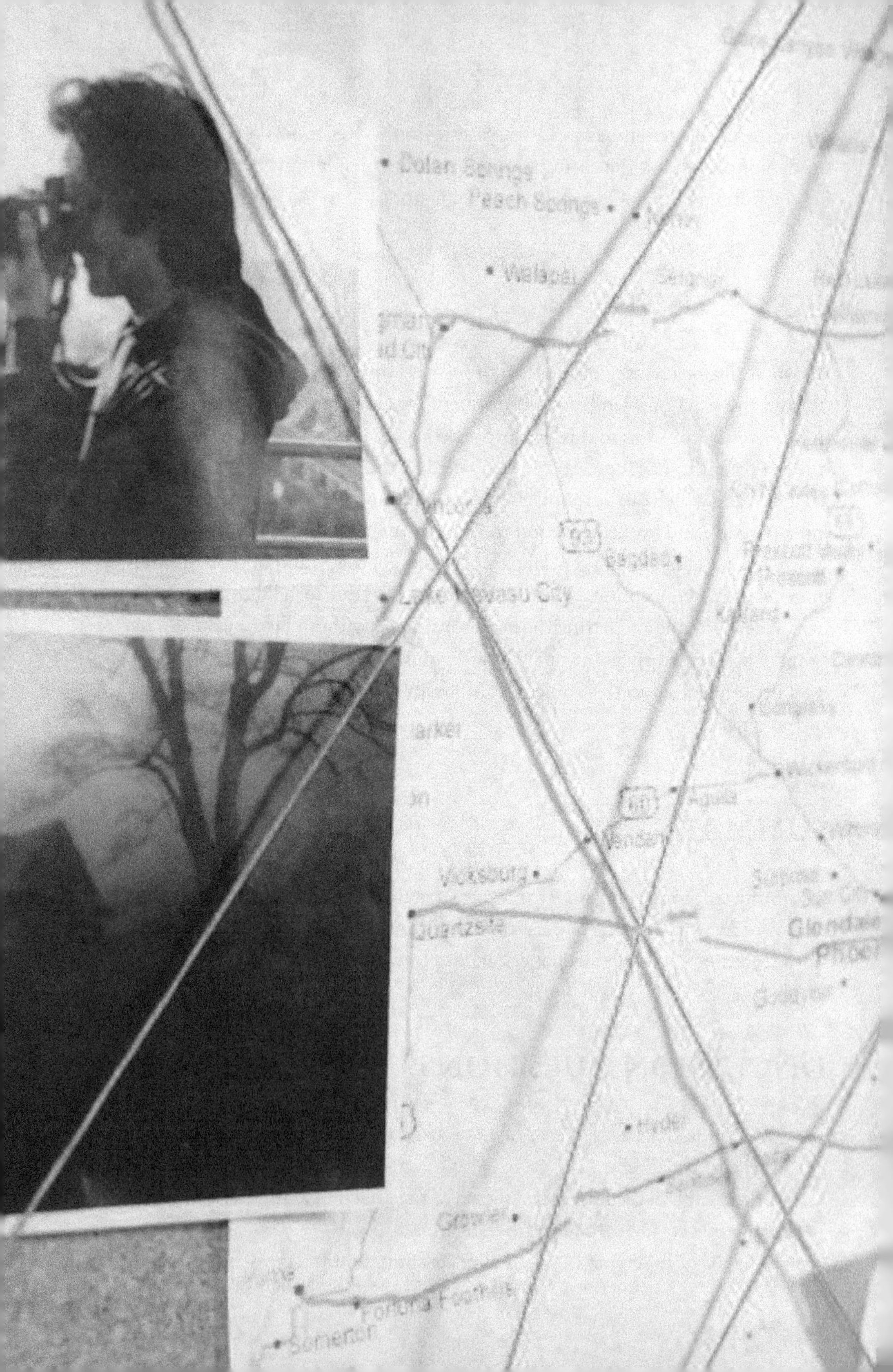
Dolan Springs
Peach Springs
Bagdad
Vicksburg
Quartzsite
Glendale

CHAPTER 10.

GENERAL ISSUES IN EYEWITNESS EVIDENCE

CHAPTER OVERVIEW

Discussions in this chapter focus on what general issues can or may have an impact on eyewitness evidence. Examples include anxiety, prior expectations and the intervening thoughts of the witness, gender, age, training, and effects of intoxication on the eyewitness. There are additional psychological and physiological aspects of the event itself to be discussed: its duration, detail salience, stress, event's violence, and witness perceptual activity. A brief look at how the eyes process light and then move into speeds and distances is presented.

Finally, some of the most important areas of this subject, post-event information are discussed. These are issues that occur after the event. The overall tone of this section concerns how information received after the event can affect memory. These changes in memory can later become "reality" for the witness!

OBJECTIVES

To teach the reader how to...

- Describe the memory process.
- Identify how anxiety, expectations, and viewpoint can affect a witness's perception.
- Identify how exposure time, detail salience, stress, and degree of violence can affect a witness's perception.
- Define the term dark adaptation.
- Identify how post-event information and altering memory can affect a witness's recollection of an event.

THE BACKGROUND

The issues raised in this section might be considered at the beginning of the background phase of the investigation. What do things that are important in the background phase mean? Assume an interviewer has a witness that he wishes to talk to. It would be beneficial to know what issues might have existed prior to the event occurring before talking to the witness. Things like the witness's expectations, people he or she has seen before, prior knowledge that might increase a witness's attention to certain details, etc., might be considered important to know prior to discussing the event. Other issues, such as the violence of the event, duration of the event, frequency, angle of view, etc., would be important to discuss when the interviewer gets to the point of the event itself. Discussed in this section are issues that attach to the witness and/or are exclusive to the event itself. Event issues will apply depending on what actually happens. These will be discussed in the next section. A later section will discuss issues that can occur after the event.

The Memory Process

As it concerns eyewitness evidence, the experts define the memory process in three phases –acquisition, retention, and retrieval. The first is the acquisition phase, which as its name implies, concerns the acquiring of the information. This is where information is encoded and placed into the memory. Visual aspects that should be attended to are considered; eye fixation and smaller and finer decisions are all made in this phase. The retention stage is the time between the acquiring of the information (basically the time of the event itself) and the time that it is retrieved from memory. The retrieval phase is where the recalled information is retrieved, for example, when one asks the witness about the event. These three terms will come up throughout the remainder of the book.

General Anxiety

As might be expected, the overall general anxiety in a person's life can negatively impact that witness's accuracy. There are tests to determine this. There is an eyewitness-testimony test wherein subjects are shown a mock crime and then asked a series of questions about details of the crime. The witness's overall ability to perceive and recall is measured. Then there is a self-preoccupation scale that measures the degree to which a witness is preoccupied by task-irrelevant thoughts. People who show a higher level of anxiety overall tend to be more preoccupied in general and tend to do worse on the aforementioned eyewitness-testimony task test. There is a life stress test that determines what negative experiences (divorce, death of a loved one, etc.) the witness has experienced in the past year and to what extent he or she was affected by it. An overall anxiety test asks questions about how a witness feels at the moment, e.g. desperate, calm, agitated. Scores are generated and interpreted accordingly. If psychologists have designed tests to determine these things, it might be worth consideration when talking to the witness. Of course, this needs to be balanced with concerns for the privacy of the witness.

Expectations

There are four general expectations to watch, for that can distort perception. The distortion might then be stored in the memory of the event consistent with each expectation.

Cultural Expectations

There are cultural expectations that are held by many people within a given culture. Some might be thought of as stereotypes. Another possibility might be, for example, a drugstore that is in the middle of the block, later being recalled as the "corner" drugstore (that it was recalled as on the corner instead, consistent with that common expectation).

Past Experiences

These expectations are from past experience. In one study, people that were shown red aces of spades did not recognize them because they were used to seeing them as black. When later asked to recall the suit, some recalled the color of the suit as something in between red and black, e.g. purple!

Personal Prejudices

Personal prejudices are narrower and consider prior persons, situations, or events.

Temporary Biases

Temporary biases might be best explained by an example. A deer hunter is out in the woods and hears rustling in the bushes. Because he expects to find a deer in the bushes, he shoots in the direction of the rustling sound while never actually knowing what was there. It was his temporary bias that led him to conclude and act in the way that he did.

In another example, people were given a set of words that didn't make sense. One of the words was "wharl." The subjects in the test may have heard the word "whale." However, if told beforehand that the nonsense word pertained to travel or transportation, these subjects would hear the word "wharf."

There are many studies and examples of temporary bias too numerous to list here. Temporary biases become more complicated when the dimension of time is added. As memory weakens over time, it is replaced by one's prior expectations. Therefore, it is important to consider the expectations the witness had of the event prior to it occurring. Evidence of prior expectations should be investigated during the discussion of the event.

The "Thoughts" of a Witness

This subject does not concern the witness who is deliberately lying or issues of suggestibility. This subject is based on the internal thoughts, wishes, and desires of that witness. A witness may have an interest in the outcome of the case, e.g. the victim of a car crash suing the one responsible for paying damages. If that victim, also a witness, is suing, the memory of the speed that the car was going might increase, in time, without any conscious intent to deceive.

People tend to remember themselves as more favorable, more attractive, and more competent or honest than the average person. People also tend to remember what they want to; if forgetting or altering an event might make it more bearable, this might be what the witness will do. In addition to the above, there are three other areas commonly known to affect memory. They are labeling, guessing, and forgetting.

Labeling

Labeling can have a dramatic impact on what a person later remembers. In a study, people were shown nonsensical figures. One figure was two circles connected by a line. Of two test subjects, one was not told anything about the figure, another was told that it was a pair of sunglasses. The subject that was told nothing was better able to recreate the actual figure whereas the other subject drew what appeared more to be sunglasses.

Guessing

A guess, if repeated over time, can make the witness more confident as being a "correct" response. This is especially problematic when the witness begins to believe that he or she is recalling from "real memory."

Forgetting

There is a thing called the forgetting curve that was first created by a German named Ebbinghaus. In his experiment, he discovered that people forget things soon after they learn them and then forgetting becomes more gradual. Another study showed the same basic curve. Recognition of pictures after about two hours was 100% but dropped to only 57% after four months (57% would be near the same response one would get by mere guessing as it concerned this study). It should be noted that not all forgetting "curves" will look the same and that many factors can come into play.

Some of the reasons cited for forgetting are that the information was never stored in the first place, sometimes interference prevents the memory from making it to the conscious level, and other times the witness is temporarily unable to retrieve the information from memory. There are also things called "constructive forces" that can be at work here. People take bits and pieces of their experience and put them together to create something that never happened.

Witness Gender and Age

The results of these studies are varied. Some show women are better eyewitnesses; some show no difference at all. Some studies suggest that women and men pay more attention to things that catch their interest. For example, women are more accurate and less suggestible with things that are traditionally female-oriented whereas the opposite is true for male-oriented items (where it concerns females).

As for age, it is intuitive that the older the child gets, the better accuracy he or she will have when recalling correct information from memory. In a study, it was found that 17-year-olds had an accuracy rate of 79% in the recognition of faces, whereas 12-year-olds had a rate of 72%. What factors determine this? It has been suggested that the older subject will have an increased ability to discriminate and will guess less often. Also, younger children are highly suggestible and can be influenced by subtle changes in question-wording. They may also be less critical when filling in gaps in memory.

With advanced age, some people decline as to accuracy while others do not. Certain tasks also appear to decline, such as memory, but often cognitive abilities remain. In a study, a dramatic falloff in accuracy occurred for those over 65 years of age (after viewing a short, violent film clip). But this is cautioned by the fact that these rely on averages; it may not apply to an elderly witness.

Training

The research suggests that training provides little or no increased ability when it comes to the ability of that witness to recall what was seen earlier. Many people consider the police officer to be a "trained" witness - more reliable and accurate. But there are studies to suggest that this is not the case. In one, 24 police officers and 154 civilians were shown a street scene and asked to watch for various people and acts. It turns out that when it comes to the detection of people and acts, the officers had no increase in ability over the civilians. In fact, the study showed that the officers picked a higher incident of false thefts than the civilians. In another study, 20 people were given a 3-day course to improve their standard abilities of recognition. They were then asked to see if they could recognize faces they had previously viewed. The results showed that the training course provided no increase in the ability to recognize faces.

This area of training is unsettled. Some witnesses who have certain types of training might pay attention to characteristics common to that training. For example, a police officer might zero in on a person entering a store wearing a heavy jacket on a hot day. The officer knows that this is a possible indication of theft, an indication that may not be picked up by a layperson, hence, the increased ability to note the jacket. But other more mundane facts may not give the same result.

Drugs and Alcohol

There are significant effects on abilities with drugs and alcohol as might be expected. Because drugs have a different impact on individual users, they will have some varying impacts on eyewitness reliability and accuracy. For alcohol, research shows that the consumption of two to three drinks appears to interfere with the formation of new memories (or the acquisition phase as mentioned above). The retrieval process (asking the witness for what they remember about the event) appears to remain intact.

Marijuana also affects the ability of the memory process. The amount of marijuana ingested also determines these abilities as well. It is said that even with socially used doses of marijuana, it can conservatively be concluded that it will affect the acquisition of information into memory. This is true even when the subject is later asked to recall that event when sober.

Benzodiazepines like diazepam (Valium) or alprazolam (Xanax) are used for the reduction of anxiety and tension. These drugs have been shown to have a negative impact on the storage of information in memory. This might seem counter-intuitive because, as discussed above, anxiety hurts eyewitness abilities, i.e. that the reduction of anxiety by these drugs would then help. But they do not.

Medical Issues

Does the witness wear glasses, contacts, or other visual aid? Does the witness suffer from an eye disease such as macular degeneration or glaucoma-related deficiencies in vision? The ability of the witness to accurately take in visual aspects of an event is obviously key to determining reliability of the witness's statements.

Lighting and Visual Interference

How much light was present at various locations and times during the event? Are light sources at a particular angle, location, or in a particular color? What time of day was it and how might weather have affected the scene? Fog, wind-blown dirt, smoke, and other interference may affect the visual clarity available to the witness.

Cross-Racial Identification

Cross-racial identification is an issue where members of one race attempt to identify members of another race. It has been shown by many experiments that members of one race are better at recognizing the faces of people in their own race than those of other races. This is true whether the person is African American, Asian American, Caucasian or other. In some studies, this does not occur to such an extent with people who have exposure to another race. For example, if a white person spends a lot of time in the African-American community, he or she would have an easier time recognizing African Americans.

Unconscious Transference

Unconscious transference occurs when the witness has displaced one person into memory for another. In one case, a ticket agent who had been robbed later identified a sailor as the man who robbed her. However, the sailor had an unbreakable alibi. It turns out the ticket agent had sold tickets to the sailor on several occasions prior to the rape and had unconsciously transferred that memory of him to one of the robbery subjects. This phenomenon can also occur with objects. Of course, it is very difficult to say whether an unconscious transference has in fact occurred. Either way, it might be a good idea to inquire if the witness has seen the person or object before the event or after the event.

What People Look at Most in a Face

Several studies have ventured to find out what people look at the most in a face. They found that three dimensions were most important: facial age (such as the presence of age lines), facial shape (e.g. long or round), and facial hair (e.g. length or style). This goes against most of people's views that the eyes are very important.

Voice Identification

There is also an issue of voice identification or the "earwitness." This is often brought up in cases of hooded robberies, obscene phone calls, bomb threats, etc. Researchers seem to agree that the same issues follow here with eyewitness evidence. In a study on age, here, over age 40, the subjects were not as accurate as young adults. These researchers also considered the issue of whether or not the blind were better. There was a small but significant difference in performance. It did not seem to matter, though, as to the amount of blindness (partially or fully impaired). It has also been shown that people are better at recognizing the voice of someone they have conversed with, as opposed to someone that they have just listened to (e.g. eavesdropped). These are only some of the potential issues here.

ISSUES INHERENT TO THE EVENT

Issues raised in this section concern the actual event itself. As said, other issues from other chapters could certainly come into play. Issues of violence of an event, light and dark adaptation, frequency and duration of an event, etc. are all considered. It is recommended you visit the scene to get a feel for it. This seems obvious but often the obvious is overlooked. You should try to recreate the time and conditions that the eyewitness experienced during the event. Also note obstructions to view (trees, bushes, etc.) and strong sunlight or dark areas. It is possible to obtain a superior understanding of the "scene" by doing so. You will probably have more time and will view it under more favorable circumstances than the witness did.

Exposure Time

Exposure time is one factor that can increase eyewitness ability. The longer the person has seen the event or object, the better the recollection. This also seems obvious, but it is always nice to get back it up with research, especially if the issue could be raised in court. One study tested this specifically. A group of subjects were shown a face and then, 8 minutes later, asked to identify the face from a series of 150 slides. Those that saw the face for 32 seconds picked the face correctly 58% of the time while those that only saw it for 10 seconds did so 48% of the time. It proved the obvious but helps put it into perspective. It should also be noted that other studies have shown that the frequency one has seen or heard something will increase later recall.

Another interesting issue here is that people tend to over-estimate the time duration of an event. This could be of great consequence to crimes like homicide. The longer the time it took the defendant to kill the victim, the more intent it implied that the defendant had. If the witness remembers a shorter time duration, the homicide might be in the "heat of passion" which may result in finding the defendant liable only for manslaughter. A longer estimate by the witness, the crime might be in cold blood and deliberate, grounding liability for first-degree murder. A longer-time estimate by the witness, then, can be critical. Another bit of research points this up even more. When an event is violent and a person is stressed, he or she will over-estimate even further. There are many other studies supporting this conclusion.

Detail Salience

Detail salience concerns those things that catch people's attention more readily than others. They are also things that will have a higher probability of being spontaneously mentioned. The following are things that help: visible for longer periods of time, center of view, large, bright, in motion, or highly active. Also, things that are colorful, extraordinary, unusual, or interesting will catch individual's attention. Conversely, things that are routine, commonplace, or insignificant will not. In a study, scores of accuracy and completeness were highest for salient items (98%) and lower for less salient (70%).

Stress

Stress can be thought of in terms of the typical bell curve (known as the Yerkes-Dodson law after the two psychologists who discovered it). That is, there is a lack of witness accuracy, or mistakes in what the witness reports, as compared to what occurred during the event, during low levels of stress, and then the accuracy rises as the stress level increases. This is probably due to the increased level of overall alertness. However, as the stress level increases, whether pleasant or unpleasant, the accuracy drops again. This can be due to an attention narrowing that occurs, a narrowing to the central theme of the event, with less attention being paid to peripheral details. This can also be dependent on what type of task is being performed during the stress. For example, a well-learned habit will have less impact on eyewitness accuracy than something that has never been attempted before. Possible issues for an interviewer to consider here might be how the witness felt (how stressed) and, if the witness was performing some type of task, had he or she done it before.

The Violence of an Event

As might be expected, the violence of an event is a major issue. Eyewitness abilities will be lessened here. This is very likely due to the increased stress that occurs (see the discussion of stress above). A study showed subjects a video of a woman having her purse snatched (in a violent manner) and another of a man asking a woman only for directions. The accuracy was consistently poorer for the violent situation. It is interesting to note that even the period just prior to an event can be impacted. In a study, subjects were shown a violent event of a boy being shot in the face. Not only was the event information impaired but also the time two minutes prior to the violent part. This has been called "retrograde amnesia" and is thought to be caused by an interference of the memory process necessary for full storage in a person's memory.

There are occasions where parts of an emotional event are remembered well. This has to do with the selectivity or narrowing of attention. Here, the main theme or central details of the event are zeroed in on other less important details. In another study, the effect of "memory freezing" is researched. Here, the issue is raised that an emotional or violent event can be rehearsed in the mind of the witness (repeatedly) causing that information to "freeze" into place. This can also occur with inaccurate information as well.

Perceptual Activity

Perceptual activity that a witness engages in while the event occurs can also impact eyewitness reliability. Much of this is common sense. In a study, they found that there was greater accuracy of identification if the item stolen was expensive and the crime serious. Accuracy was 56% here. If the crime was not serious and the item was not expensive, the accuracy rate dropped to 19%. It is important that this information be known prior to the event taking place for this to be the case, e.g. that the witness is aware that an item is expensive prior to the crime occurring. In sum, if one knows something about an event before it occurs, it can influence how they view it, what they pay attention to, and how much attention they give to various details.

Weapon Focus

There is a phenomenon known as weapon focus. Here, as might be imagined, the eyewitness is more likely to notice the gun and less likely the facial features or other features of the assailant. This does not limit itself to guns - it can be a knife, club, etc. There have been many studies that compare mock events where, in one, a weapon was used and, in another, something innocuous was used (most other aspects being the same). The research supports the conclusion that in the event where the weapon was used, the "witnesses" were less accurate (when asked to identify things other than the weapon) than witnesses in the non-weapon event. Some studies have even tracked eye fixation in similar cases and have found that fixation occurs earlier and for a longer duration on the weapon than on other benign things.

Dark Adaptation

There is an interesting issue called dark adaptation. There are receptor cells in the eye - rods and cones. The signals that come from these cells are eventually received into the brain. The rods mediate nighttime or low-intensity vision while the cones deal with high-intensity and color (wavelength). Therefore, less color is seen in the moonlight because there is not enough light to stimulate the cones. Also, rods do not provide as sharp an image as cones do, hence nighttime vision depicts objects as coarse and with a lack of definition. The ability to adapt to darkness will take the cones about 5 minutes (in humans) and the rods about 30 minutes, depending on the duration and intensity of light that they were recently (previously) exposed to. Some people always have an inability to see in the dark (called "night blindness"). Several things can cause this, but the most common is an inability to process vitamin A. Sometimes a doctor will prescribe an increased intake of vitamin A. It might be worth asking the witness if their doctor has done so.

If a person claims to have seen color at night, this should be looked at with some scrutiny. This is because there is very little light to stimulate the cones, the receptors that process color (wavelength). Rods are used much more for night vision and they do not process color. Some people are completely color blind, seeing only black, white, and shades of gray. Others are partially color blind, lacking one of the three color pigments usually found in the cones. Most common are those that are red-green blind; they see things in shades of blue and yellow. Less common is blue-yellow blindness; they see shades of red-green. Color blindness is more common in males than in females and diseases like glaucoma and diabetes can disturb color vision. Alcoholism can cause reds to appear darker than they are. After the age of 50, changes in the lens of the eye cause blues to look darker than they are, causing confusion with greens.

There is also a thing called "light adaptation." Here, after a light has been turned on in a room once dark, the eyes will adjust much more quickly, generally between a few seconds to fifteen seconds. This is much faster than the eyes adjust, as in the dark adaptation above.

Speed and Distance

Speed and distance are difficult for people to properly estimate. In a very early study on distance, subjects were asked to estimate the distance between two buildings. The actual distance was 310 feet, but the average estimate was 346 feet (the range was much wider; some estimated much higher, creating that average).

Speed creates a similar problem. This is often a big issue in car accident cases. In a study, subjects were told in advance that they were going to be questioned about the speed of a vehicle. Though it only went 12 mph, estimates were between 10 and 50 mph. It is also interesting to note that large objects appear to be going slower than smaller ones. Perhaps this accounts for the reason people over-estimate motorcycle speeds and why large trains hit people who underestimate the train's speed while they are attempting to cross the tracks.

ISSUES IMPORTANT AFTER THE EVENT

The following information concerns issues that can come up after the event occurred. Much of it will deal with how the witness's memory can be manipulated and/or distorted. These are probably some of the more important issues that you should be concerned with. As before, these issues can bleed into other areas but are more relevant here.

The time between an event and the time it is recollected is important, especially the length of time and the type of event. The first issue is with memory loss or forgetting. As discussed (see The Background, Perceiving Events, Intervening Thoughts of a Witness), a person will quickly forget what he or she has seen. With little left in memory, what occurs between then and the time one interviews the witness is of great importance.

Post Event Information

This occurs when a witness is exposed to new information after the witnessed event. This can have a dramatic impact. In one study, some students read the account of a lecture they had attended. A news reporter had given an account of that lecture in an article. This article, however, contained errors about what was really given in the lecture. Those students who read the article made many more errors on an exam about that lecture. Those students who read the article remembered the wrong information from the article, assuming they had learned it from the instructor's original lecture!

Enhancing Memory

One can enhance memory. By simply mentioning an existing object, it is possible to increase the likelihood that it will be recalled later. In a study, subjects viewed an accident where there was no stop sign in the scene. They were asked a question whether they had seen the car that caused the accident to run "the" stop sign. When later asked to recall if there was a stop sign, 53% "remembered" seeing one. For those that were not asked this question, only 37% said they saw a stop sign.

Altering Memory

Misleading information can supplement memory, that is, place something there that was non-existent. Misinformation can also transform it (i.e. alter it). In a study, subjects had been shown an accident and in the scene, some were shown a stop sign in the intersection, and others were shown a yield sign. As an example, the people that were shown the stop sign in the mock accident were asked questions that suggested a yield sign. Many of these subjects later reported they had seen a yield sign. The stop sign was transformed in memory to a yield sign by the misleading information in the question.

In yet another study, this concept is carried one step further. Here, more general information was added, for example, that a driver was drunk. The study indicates that this suggestion might lead to other conclusions, i.e. that because the driver was drunk, he must have also run the stop sign when, in fact, he did not. When it comes to altering memory, it is much more difficult to alter salient details as opposed to peripheral details. Salient details are recalled with significantly greater accuracy and are much more difficult to alter.

Timing of Post-Event Information

The timing of post-event information is important. This concerns whether putting misleading information into a witness's mind near the event would have a greater decrease in accuracy than putting it there later.

In a study, subjects were shown slides and then given misleading information just before being asked about the slides. The subjects tended to recall the misleading information more here than if asked just after the event before the true information had a chance to fade.

It is suggested that, for effective investigation, you learn how the witness came to believe the current version of the event they are reporting. Witnesses can learn things, and hence adopt misleading information, by talking to other witnesses, from the media, and/or by questioning other investigators.

"Freezing" Effects

Remember, freezing effects occur when information is repeated many times. This can cause this information to become more solidified (or "frozen") into memory. If a witness is repeatedly questioned about an event, repeating that answer may have this effect, whether right or wrong.

In general, there are four factors that affect memory distortion:

- The time interval between the viewing of the event and its later recollection.
- The verbal form of the post-event information (heads up here).
- The violence of an event.
- Any warning given to the witness that post-event information will be distorted. In this last case, the witness must be warned immediately before it is given. If so, the witness will scrutinize the post-event information more carefully.

Context-Dependent Memory

There is a phenomenon related to emotional memories known as state-dependent memory, in which retrieval accuracy is best if the subject's cognitive state at the time of retrieval matches the cognitive state at the time the information is placed into memory.

When memories have an emotional component, retrieval may be best when the individual is induced to a corresponding emotional state (mood-dependent memory), which is done by verbally or physically placing the subject in the same context and may offer a valuable tool for probing eyewitness accounts.

CONCLUSION

This chapter saw issues that can affect the eyewitness process before an event, during an event, and after an event.

The next chapter looks at the actual interview. Certainly, every issue mentioned up until now can also be a consideration for the interview, especially post-event information. That is, what one does in the interview (e.g. suggestions or misleading information) can be considered as post-event information to a future interviewer.

SUMMARY

Many issues can affect the testimony of an eyewitness, including incidents occurring before, during, and after the actual event. It is the investigator's responsibility to identify these incidents and how they may have affected the witness' memory of the actual event.

DISCUSSION QUESTIONS

- Why is it important to understand the background of an eyewitness's testimony?
- What issues inherent in the incident may affect the witness' testimony?
- How can a witness's memory be manipulated or distorted after the event?

CHAPTER 11.

THE INTERVIEW

CHAPTER OVERVIEW

As always, be sure to do your own due diligence when it comes to which interview techniques to use. This is because the interview of an eyewitness can be a delicate and may have very significant consequences for others. Research and laws change impacting what may be considered current for you type of case or jurisdiction. Consultation with appropriate professionals in the areas of psychology and law as well as with department or agency policy should be performed.

The interview of an eyewitness should be viewed within the context of the memory process. The interview is essentially the third component of the three stages of the memory process, retrieval; the others being acquisition and retention. The last chapter discussed how the memory process works, and how stress, anxiety, expectations, and intervening thoughts of a witness can come into play. It also saw how the issues of age, sex, training, and alcohol can all influence eyewitness testimony. Other issues of perceptions of people and things inherent to the event itself are factors as well. Most importantly, it examined the issues of post-event information and how this can affect memory.

This chapter will cover the interview environment, the type of retrieval (general question types), and the subtleties of question wording. Then it moves on to the most widely known innovative technique, the cognitive interview. This will be covered in greater detail and length than other areas because of its importance. In the interest of being thorough and complete, it also looks at very recent research that challenges the cognitive interview in some areas and compares it to simpler techniques, the structured interview and the standard interview. Next, there is a discussion about hypnosis, witness confidence, and the interviewer. Things are rounded out with the perennial lineup, whether it be in-person or by using photographs.

ENVIRONMENT

As you might expect, the environment can be important. The comfort the witness and aspects of that environment might inhibit the retrieval of valuable information from that witness. In the case of eyewitnesses, a new environment can inhibit recognition. It is suggested that the subject, where possible, be identified at the scene and in the same environment as the event or crime.

Of course, issues of suggestibility and other logistical problems need to be considered in the decision. The scene could be a dangerous place (i.e. a busy freeway or "bad" neighborhood) or it may be dissimilar in some way (i.e. the crime was seen at 3:00 am and the interviewer is unable to get out to the scene at this hour to get the similar lighting conditions). You also need to consider the passage of time and issues of forgetting, as well as to be sure you do not present a subject for identification in such a way that it could lead to suggestive or improper identification of that subject.

TYPES OF RETRIEVAL

The type of retrieval will yield differing results. More involved techniques will be discussed later, but for now, there are three general question types. There is the narrative or free report, the controlled narrative, and finally an interrogatory type of questioning (i.e. multiple choice). In the free report or narrative, the subject is simply asked to tell what happened in their own words. The controlled narrative narrows down the scope, such as, "What type of clothes was he wearing?" The interrogative is still more precise. An example might be, "Did he have dark or light hair?" The free report is generally more complete but is less accurate whereas the controlled narrative and interrogatory are less complete but more accurate. Striking a balance between the three is nothing more than the use of common sense and experience. It is suggested that the free report be used first, followed by the others. It is also suggested that the event be told as a story or chronology. If used in court, the psychological factors will probably be raised as they would occur in that chronology as well. It is better, in court and to a jury, to express these theories as the three-stage process of acquisition, retention, and retrieval (a chronology).

QUESTION WORDING

How a question is worded is probably one of the most volatile components of the eyewitness interview. The precise words used are crucial. The research will speak for itself. Only some of it is presented here.

In a study, subjects were asked to watch a movie. When asked, "how long was the movie?," these subjects guessed 130 minutes. Those that were asked, "how short was the movie?," guessed 100 minutes! Also in this research, in another scenario, subjects were asked how many other products they had tried than the ones being asked about (here, over-the-counter medicine). The ones that were asked "1? 2? 3?" other products as suggestions said, on average, they had tried 3.3 other products. Those that were asked "1? 5? 10?" averaged 5.2!

In another study, subjects were asked to view a mock accident. Certain subjects were asked if they had seen "a" broken headlight, and others were asked if they had seen "the" broken headlight. Of course, there was no broken headlight. The ones who were asked "the" had responded much more often that they had seen the headlight; something that was not even there.

In yet another experiment, subjects were asked questions about a film of a car accident they had seen. Those that were asked a question where the word "smashed" was used in the question (as to the colliding of the cars) came up with the highest speed estimates of the speed of the cars. Those that were asked with "collided" came up with lower estimates of speed and those asked with "contacted" were lower still.

Even the location of a word in a sentence can impact the witness's memory." If the misleading information is buried in a minor clause, it has a greater likelihood of being adopted unknowingly into the witness's memory. If it is the focus of a question, it is more likely to be noticed and discarded as misinformation. For example, if asked, "Was the small car blue or green?," it is less likely that the witness would notice the suggestion that the car was small (misinformation) than if asked, "Was the car, that was small, blue or green?" It might be good, then, to show the interview in a transcript (verbatim) that you did not have any misinformation, or that if one did, it would have been more obvious to the witness (who would then have noticed and discarded it).

Questions should be phrased, where possible, in such a way that they will not elicit an answer that the witness will perceive as being threatening to his or her self-image. People tend to distort their memory in a way that favors their self-image. They tend to see themselves as more intelligent or better-looking than the average person. It may not be enough to have established a good rapport. If a possible answer might be threatening, it may cause the memory that the answer was drawn from to distort in favor of a positive self-image, i.e. asking, "Did you remember, like all the other witnesses, the color of the car?," might cause the witness to invent a color simply to appear as observant as the other witnesses.

What of the ability to tell if there has been a memory alteration or not? In a study, subjects were asked to watch a mock accident. A comparison of the two groups was made. One group was NOT given misleading questions and where a stop sign was shown in the mock accident. Another group had received misleading questions and was not shown stop sign. Some differences were noted between the groups. The ones that were given misleading questions tended to use more words to describe what they had seen (because a witness uses a lot of words for description does not necessarily mean they have an accurate account). They also tended to describe its function. Those who actually saw a sign and had no misleading questions tended to describe more specific features (i.e. its color or shape). However, it is ultimately very difficult to tell whether a memory is real or not.

NON-VERBAL INFLUENCES

Even non-verbal influences can have an impact. This includes tone of voice, gaze, posture, and movements of the head and eyes, etc. In a study, teachers were told that certain students were smart and others were not smart (when in fact they were picked at random). It was shown that those students who were labeled as smart actually increased in performance over the other children. It was postulated that the teachers gave non-verbal signals which these students picked up on, causing performance to change.

This can be found more specifically in eyewitness cases where the police show a witness a picture of the subject. The witness may simply believe that the police have already found the right person. If any interviewer shows more zeal, or lack of it, in the direction of a potential conclusion, this may influence what is later recalled. It could also occur when one witness expresses confidence in his or her own identification in the presence of a to-be-influenced witness. This is one reason why it is best to interview witnesses separately.

THE COGNITIVE INTERVIEW

There is an interview technique called the cognitive interview. It was developed by two psychologists, Ronald P. Fisher, Ph.D. of the Florida International University, and R. Edward Geiselman, Ph.D. of the University of California at Los Angeles. They present the technique in their book, Memory Enhancing Techniques for Investigative Interviewing [Charles C. Thomas Publisher, Springfield, Ill., 1992]. We offer below a synopsis of some of the contents of the book. Though the technique is relatively straightforward, it is better to obtain this book and follow its directions for the performance of the actual interview.

In the book, the authors provide a training schedule that will allow investigators to practice and enhance their skills in the use of this interview technique. The following is a brief overview of the technique itself. Because this is one of the more widely known techniques, this area deserves a little more attention than the other areas discussed in their book.

It is worth pointing out that there is some overlap here and what was discussed above. This interview technique draws from other areas of discipline and other parts are universal techniques that will be used in virtually any type of interview.

It is presented as a summary below and in the same order the authors do. However, it is not intended as an exhaustive discussion of what the book contains. The book starts with the dynamics of the interview.

DYNAMICS OF THE INTERVIEW

The eyewitness is the one with all the information. The witness is encouraged to take an active and central role in this process. This is done by asking the witness directly to do so or by merely asking open-ended questions (which will elicit an open-ended response). Interrupting the witness is not recommended. Also, a good rapport needs to be established. This is done by personalizing the interview (active listening, treating the witness as an individual) and creating communication empathy (understanding things from the witness's perspective and communicating this understanding). The interviewer and witness goals need to be brought together, as each can differ. Each should continue to generate, as a common goal, as much relevant information as possible. Through a process called "synchrony," the interviewer can create a desired behavior in the witness. People tend to mirror the other person's behavior. By behaving as the interviewer wishes the witness to behave, they can better control what the witness does (e.g. if the interviewer relaxes, the witness will relax). These are all part of the dynamics of the interview.

OVERCOMING EYEWITNESS LIMITATIONS

Initially, a witness's anxiety needs to be controlled, as the event witnessed is often unsettling. Anxiety does not help information retrieval. There are various methods here which include helping the witness understand that the anxiety is normal, and to relax and breathe slowly, and perhaps to describe the event as though it were happening to someone else. Stressful questions might be saved at the end of the interview. A witness's confidence should be kept high and they should be encouraged not to withhold any information (even if it seems trivial or contradictory). Of course, this should not be at the expense of fabrication or uncertainty (the witness should be explicitly told this).

There are various methods used to facilitate the memory process, e.g. showing the witness pictures or sketches to facilitate recognition. Issues of suggestibility and expectation should be considered though. The witness should be told to provide as detailed information as they are able. They can even draw pictures of a crime scene or act out the actions of the subject. "Person" features should be emphasized, especially facial features and odd characteristics of a subject (or the most distinctive feature). If the witness provides a subjective response, the interviewer can provide a more objective version, with a rephrasing of this back to the witness. Ultimately, though, subjective responses can be hard to interpret and translate.

LOGISTICS OF INTERVIEWING

Interviews should be conducted with one eyewitness at a time, if possible. Ultimately, the interview itself should be done where there are as few distractions as possible. Various issues can come up in the home, at the office, or at the crime scene if this is where the interview is conducted. Remote interviews are not suggested for the initial interview, but might be good for follow-ups. The interview should be done as soon after the event as possible so that the witness does not forget. This should be balanced, of course, with the issue of residual anxiety (as anxiety is detrimental to the information retrieval process). The interviewer should also make an effort to increase the length of the interview. If not, the witness should be encouraged to provide information to the investigator that may occur to the witness after the interview has been terminated. The witness should be asked to contact the interviewer if new information is remembered. A follow-up interview several days later is encouraged.

MECHANICS OF THE INTERVIEW

It is suggested that the interviewer uses neutral, non-leading questions, in simple and easy-to-understand terms. As discussed earlier, question-wording can have a dramatic impact on witness testimony. It is suggested that open-ended questions precede closed questions and that open-ended questions are preferred, in general, to other types. The interviewer should speak in a slow and calm tone of voice, waiting a few seconds, following a response before asking another question. The use of recorders and shorthand notes can help increase the interviewer's concentration and reduce the need for interruptions.

PRINCIPLES OF COGNITION

The event that was remembered is not only stored as factual observations but also as the physiological, psychological, and environmental contexts in which the event was experienced. Events are recorded at different levels of detail, the most detailed information being the hardest for the interviewer and witness to coax out of memory. These events can be stored in different mental "codes" and are also represented as a string of features that can be retrieved independently of others. The two types of codes are image codes, which are generally more accurate, and concept codes, which are less accurate but easier to retrieve from memory. Image codes store an event as sensory images, usually visual but can also include auditory, smell, touch, and taste. Concept codes are usually listed as a series of meaningful concepts, like storage in a dictionary. A subject might be thought of as tall, greedy, loud, or threatening - all qualities called up with the concept of the subject.

There are three principles used to enhance memory: focused concentration (informing the witness that the process is mentally difficult and giving overall encouragement), context reinstatement (placing the witness back in the same psychological, physiological, emotional, and environmental context), and multiple retrieval attempts (witness should be encouraged to do as many attempts as might appear necessary).

PRACTICAL TECHNIQUES TO FACILITATE MEMORY

Here, the recreation of the original context is discussed. There are various techniques offered here, e.g. showing the witness a non-leading photo of the scene, instructing the witness to think about the context, etc. Similar issues such as the witness maintaining their concentration, encouraging the witness through the mentally difficult process, and not interrupting the witness are stressed as vital.

WITNESS-COMPATIBLE QUESTIONING

In addition, mental images of the event are directly or indirectly probed. The mental record of the event is obtained by either directly asking the witness or by listening to a narration given by the witness and inferring mental images from the narration. A strategy for finding and probing the mental images with the most detailed descriptions should be developed. Because of the mental concentration required, the images with the most detail for a particular question are asked about first (this is known as the Principle of Detail).

Also, the strategy is to stay in the same mental image for as long as possible (the Principle of Momentum). As such, questions should be ordered so as to stay within the same image. This is because the witness is better able to reach more information by staying in an image and concentrating on it (e.g. when describing a face, get all the information about that before moving on to the shoes). This is also due to the fact that shifting from one image to another is mentally fatiguing. The optimal strategy here will produce optimal retrieval of relevant and useful facts for an investigation.

PROBING IMAGE AND CONCEPT MEMORY CODES

For image codes, the interviewer is told to use the same words used by the witness in earlier interviews to describe the event, if possible. The witness is told to view the image vividly and clearly first, before discussing it verbally. Questions should be open-ended and asked in a slow and deliberate manner. Detailed and elaborate responses should be requested. Concept codes are probed by asking the witness to imagine the event from someone else's perspective or by going through the event in various orders (e.g. remembering it backward).

The next chapters in their book discuss the chronology of the cognitive interview and also provide sample interviews with comments where suggestions are given and where errors are pointed out. The final chapter is a training program for learning the cognitive interview. The main issue, as with any interview technique, is practice, practice, practice!

CHALLENGES TO THE COGNITIVE INTERVIEW AND OTHER ALTERNATIVES

The cognitive interview is not the only method used to interview eyewitnesses. In fact, there is recent research suggests that this cognitive interview may not be significantly better than other interview types (techniques) and may even be less effective if used inappropriately, e.g. without proper training. An article appeared in Psychology, a refereed journal sponsored by the American Psychological Association, raises some of these issues. Its authors, Memon and Stevenage, look at other techniques and compare them to the cognitive interview. Note that there has been other research and treatment focusing on the cognitive interview, but this article appears to be helpful in understanding the context of how eyewitness interviewing is not an exacting science.

Before getting to the article, it is worthwhile to define the two interview techniques.

THE STANDARD INTERVIEW AND THE STRUCTURED INTERVIEW

The first is the standard interview. This is the one most investigators and police officers use. This involves essentially having the witness tell the interviewer about the witnessed event, like a story (a chronology - from beginning to end). The question type is usually an open-ended question (or free report) followed by more specific and controlled questions to elicit responses. Then there is the structured interview. This carries the standard interview one step further. It adds "communicative" components, which include rapport building (placing the control of the interview with the witness rather than the interviewer) and a questioning strategy that is guided by the witness's free report rather than some other formalized strategy.

This article, which looks at the cognitive interview, points out many issues. This section will discuss only the main points and it will avoid the more technical aspects of the article. The first thing that is foremost important is that the success of the cognitive interview is based on comparisons of this interview to untrained interviewers. Results with the cognitive interview were obviously higher here (45% better). However, when compared to the structured interview, the results were not the same. Note that the structured interview and the cognitive interview make use of the same techniques of rapport building, communicative techniques, and transfer of control to the witness. But, the cognitive interview adds the cognitive tools of context reinstatement, reporting in detail, multiple retrieval, and imagery (as mentioned above). To what extent do these cognitive strategies increase eyewitness performance? Research suggests that the cognitive interview is only beneficial for the first time the witness is questioned. Successive retrieval attempts (interviews) showed no advantage in the cognitive interview over the structured interview, where it concerned additional gains in information. A study by Memon et al, had two groups, one used the cognitive interview and one used the structured interview (both groups had received extensive training in their respective techniques). There were no differences between the two techniques (where adult witnesses were used) for the overall amount of recalled, accuracy of recall, and number of errors. There are some studies that show a favor towards the cognitive interview.

There are also motivational issues here as well which affect both the interviewer and the witness. Trained interviewers show an increase in motivation to be successful and to prove that the training has worked. This can cause them to ask more questions, probe more and create a demanding environment where the witness feels compelled to say more (some of which may not be accurate). This would be true, however, for any training that the interviewer receives, cognitive or structured.

The authors also point out that witnesses who have witnessed a stressful event may not want to recall the event in the way that the cognitive interview requires. Though Fisher and Geiselman (the creators of the cognitive interview) do mention that one should not interview witnesses that are not cooperative, it is not always clear when this is the case. Where memory recall is difficult or unfavorable to the witness, this will probably cause the interviewer to start using leading questions or prompts to get the ball rolling. This runs the risk, as with any leading question or strategy, of creating errors in recall as a result of the leading questions. Also, though the cognitive interview increases the overall amount of information, this is at the expense of an increase in errors. The authors point to a similar cause as that found in hypnosis (as to increased error rate).

Another possible reason for the increased error rate is the social pressure to give a desired response (based on the training issue mentioned above). It is not clear that the cognitive interview itself is the cause of this, however. The increase might be due to an increase in detailed probing by the cognitive interviewer (this type of questioning typically increases error rates). It may also be due to the imagery techniques which, when used in isolation, can increase the number of errors.

The authors noted that the cognitive interview increased errors but not confabulations. Errors are alterations in what has already been stored in memory (that a blue shirt is remembered in error as green) whereas a confabulation is the creation of something that was never there (remembering a third subject where there were only two).

Also, the authors feel that the benefits outweigh the risks, that is, the increase in overall information outweighs the number of errors.

Finally, the cognitive and structured interviews have the same accuracy rates. However, because of the above issues of errors, the authors suggest that a more cautious approach than the cognitive interview be used where the accuracy of small details is critical.

HYPNOSIS

Hypnosis research indicates that there are some risks in using this with eyewitnesses and should be used only in limited circumstances. Courts in many jurisdictions do not even allow testimony obtained by hypnosis. Still, others allow it in only limited circumstances. Most research shows that hypnosis rarely improves memory and makes the witness more susceptible to post-event suggestions. Hypnosis may provide an increase in overall information, but this will be at the expense of an increase in false information as well. Finally, hypnosis might increase the confidence the witness has in his or her account without any corresponding increase in actual accuracy.

Proponents of hypnosis will argue that it only be used to generate leads, which can then be corroborated with other evidence. They also say that hypnosis increases concentration, increases relaxation (beneficial to memory retrieval), and enhances a trusting relationship with the interviewer (hypnotist). The arguments for use of hypnosis ultimately should be judged on a case-by-case basis, taking into account all the issues presented.

THE INTERVIEWER

It is a good idea to find out who has previously interviewed the witness. When you speak to the witness, it can be helpful to reconstruct the identification process used with that witness up to that point in time. Mostly, you will be looking for issues of post-event information and leading questions (this will be especially true with children). This issue is magnified with people of authority and status, as they can more easily manipulate and persuade others.

Other issues should also be explored. For example, has this witness identified the wrong person before, or has there been any other indication of inconsistent identifications or failures to identify, e.g. the witness has viewed the subject and failed to identify? Other issues to look for might be any in-person, or photo lineups the witness has viewed or other indication to the witness that the defendant or subject, for example, may have committed the act. Also, look for obstructions to view (obstacles, lighting conditions, etc.) that might contradict prior witness statements.

Finally, as with any interview technique, it is always good to be sure you and the witness are using the same definition of a word. This seems obvious, but has caught investigators on more than a few occasions. Any word that is ambiguous, especially adjectives, is fair game (e.g. fast, suspicious, old or new, etc.). When taking the statement, it is best to write the descriptors exactly as the witness has stated them.

WITNESS CONFIDENCE

A common misconception is that an increase in confidence of a witness's recollections means that the witness must be accurate in his or her account. The research is all over the place here. Some show a correlation between confidence and accuracy, others show just the opposite (increased confidence shows an inaccurate account), and others still show no correlation either way. The bottom line here is that witness confidence cannot be relied upon as an indicator of witness accuracy.

One particular response should be viewed with caution. If someone tells a witness that an event has already occurred, this can lead the witness to believe that they "knew it all along" that it was going to happen. This may then be assimilated into memory. Thus, if a witness says in a response something to the effect, "I knew it all along but failed to mention it earlier," then this and any other response about that event should be scrutinized.

LINEUPS (IN-PERSON AND PHOTO)

Lineups (In-person and Photo) are a relatively involved area. Issues here can be critical. Previous editions of this book covered this topic, but it was decided to refer the reader to two resources that have been developed specifically around this area of study.

One resource is put out by the National Institutes of Justice and it goes into great detail around every aspect of the photo lineup and in-person lineup (show up). This is a free resource with thorough and in-depth information:

https://nij.ojp.gov/library/publications/eyewitness-evidence-guide-law-enforcement

Another resource is the National Research Council's reference of 2014, "Identifying the Culprit: Assessing Eyewitness Identification." (Washington, D.C.: The National Academies Press). It is available, free of charge at this link:

https://doi.org/10.17226/18891

As always, refer to legal counsel, department, or enterprise management prior to relying on these resources.

CONCLUSION

This concludes the interview part of the book. It visited the interview environment and looked at the intricacies of the question type and wording. This chapter reviewed hypnosis, the interviewer, and the area of lineups. It also took a good hard look at the most widely known technique, the cognitive interview. To make it a well-rounded discussion, it also included a summary of an article that takes a closer look at the interview technique and another possible methods.

The issues and techniques that are found in the area of the interview of the eyewitness are constantly changing and growing. It is always good to contact attorneys or psychologists who specialize in this area to get an update on what is hot and what is not.

THE INFLUENCE OF THE FORM OF A QUESTION

The sample study presented below was included to give the readers a basic idea of what a "study" looks like, how it reads, the level of depth it goes into, etc. This particular study is also one of the more interesting studies. It is often cited in today's studies and has provided some of the first inquiries into the form of a question and its influences. Though much of this study is still valid, other studies have been done that expand or modify its findings.

Note that this study was done in 1916 and this book has included it word for word; some of the spelling is different and other aspects will date it (i.e. see, 4. Description of Experiment, (a) Observation materials, and apparatus, where Muscio has to describe what a moving picture is!).

Not all the study was included here. There are another 30 pages or so (equivalent) that go into great detail about the study. This was omitted because of its length and complexity. The material presented is enough to give an overall idea of what is in a "study"; inclusion of the rest is not necessary. Cites and other references are also omitted. To see the rest, it can be viewed by visiting this site: Muscio, The Influence of the Form of a Question, 8 Brit. J. Psyc. 351-86 (1916).

THE INFLUENCE OF THE FORM OF A QUESTION

By Bernard Muscio
(From the Cambridge Psychological Laboratory)

1. Aim of the Experiment

In this paper is presented an account of part of an experiment dealing with evidence. The specific aim of the part described here was to compare certain question forms in regard to their respective influence upon answers, it is assumed, as a result of previous experiments in the psychology of evidence, that the answer to this question is under certain conditions partly determined by the question's form. Its more general aim was to obtain data from which an analysis of the various mental processes operative in determining answers to questions might be made.

Binet considered that whenever a question was put to a witness, his memory was 'forced.' He distinguished, however, between different degrees of 'forcing.' The type of certain questions rendered them, in his opinion, moderately suggestive, while other questions, for a similar reason, were strongly suggestive. The type of question considered by Binet to be moderately suggestive is fairly unambiguous. It is the question that contains a negative: "Isn't the button fastened to the card with thread?" There is a difficulty, however, in discovering what types of questions Binet meant by the unsuggestive and the strongly suggestive questions. His list of unsuggestive questions contains questions of types that have since been distinguished as different. Thus, it contains the two questions: "What color is the portrait?" and, "Is the stamp new or does it bear a postmark?" Formally, these two questions are very different. The latter is now distinguished as a 'complete disjunction' question. Similarly, his list of strongly suggestive questions contains questions of different types. For example, it contains the two questions: "At what part (of the picture) is the little dog?" and, "Has the gentleman the left leg crossed over the right one or the right one crossed over the left one?" These questions again are formally distinct in type, the latter being now designated an 'incomplete disjunction' question.

The fact is that Binet used no one principle of classification in distinguishing different types of questions, but based his distinctions partly on the question form and partly on the question content. Thus, the moderately suggestive question always contains an identical formal element, the negative, and is always concerned with something that did not occur in the observed material. The unsuggestive questions, so far as they are of any one formal type, are chiefly complete disjunction questions (with regard to which one of the alternatives offered must be true). Similarly, the strongly suggestive questions, so far as they are of one formal type, are chiefly incomplete disjunction questions; but perhaps the principal element which renders them strongly suggestive is their content. They are sometimes, e.g., preceded by a false statement concerning the observed material. The result is that Binet's work, so far as the relative importance of different question forms is concerned, is of value chiefly because of its suggestiveness.

Binet's experiments and a number of investigations of a similar general character have been carried out in Germany.

As a consequence, Binet's rough-and-ready classification of types of questions has been much improved upon, although there exists even yet no complete classification. Stern was the pioneer of the German work on evidence. He distinguished at least six types of questions. A more recent investigator, Lipmann, distinguishes seven types, as follows:

1. The determinative question forms ("The question with the question word"); e.g. What color is the shirt?
2. The complete disjunction question form; e.g., Is the child in the meadow asleep or awake?
3. The Yes-No question form; e.g., Is there a cupboard in the room?
4. The No question form; e.g. Might the man have a spoon in his hand?
5. The Yes question form; e.g., Isn't there a cupboard in the room?
6. The incomplete disjunction question form; e.g., Is the shirt red or green?
7. The implicative question form (questions with false implications); e.g., What is the child in the meadow doing? (This implies (1) that there is a meadow, (2) that there is a child in it).

It will be noticed that this classification is not made on any one principle; e.g. , most of the question types, whatever else they may be, as 'implicative.' "Is the child in the meadow asleep or awake?" (the complete disjunction question), is quite as implicative as "What is the child in the meadow doing?" In connection with the present experiment, however, no attempt has been made to elaborate on any complete classification of the question forms. A chief aim of the experiment was to investigate a distinction not hitherto noticed. Since previous classifications have not been made on any one principle, the possibility of their being complete was a mere matter of chance. And, in fact, they have not been complete. One fairly obvious and very important distinction between types of questions has been omitted from them.

This distinction is illustrated in the following manner. Consider the two questions: "Did you see a pistol on the table?" and "Was there a pistol on the table?" Outside a psychological laboratory, the aim of anyone who might ask either of these two questions would be to obtain information as to the presence of a pistol on the table. The former question, however, asks if the pistol was seen, the latter if it was there.

It is not possible, strictly speaking, to say that the two questions differ in form only, for literally they do differ also in content, even if the 'was there' interpreted by Berkeley would have interpreted it. The relation between the contents of the two questions is nonetheless very close. Both contain an identical element 'pistol on the table.' Further, when both questions are asked with regard to observed material, they may be considered having identical content, since 'Was there' may then be considered equivalent to 'Did you notice?' It is not necessary, however, to adopt a one-sided attitude here. The two questions may be asked, and the aim in asking each may be identical, namely, to obtain information about the presence of the pistol on the table. In the present experiment, questions of these two forms (or types) are compared from this point of view, that is, with regard to the character of the information yielded in answer to each so far as this information concerns 'objective fact."

In other questions of the form "Did you see....?," the specific term 'see' may be replaced by other specific terms, such as 'hear,' according to the nature of the material observed; or all specific terms may be replaced by such generic terms as 'perceive' or 'notice.'

I propose calling all questions of a type similar to that of the question, "Did you see a pistol on the table?" subjective-direction questions, since they tend primarily to direct the attention of the person who is questioned to his actual prior relation to the object; and for an analogous reason, this text proposes calling all questions of the type similar to, "Was there a pistol on the table?" (or, e.g., Did B. whistle?), objective-direction questions since they tend primarily to direct a witness's attention to the object observed, and not to his observation of it. Every question is either subjective-directive or objective-directive.

The importance of the above-stated distinction depends upon the necessity, which sometimes arises, for using leading questions. Jurists allow leading questions to be employed in certain circumstances, e.g., if a witness is hostile, or if the matter of examination is very complex (when it is assumed that the leading question will 'refresh' the memory). Although a leading question is never exactly defined, it would generally be agreed that some leading questions are more misleading than others. Thus, it would probably be agreed generally that to ask whether the coat was very tattered is more suggestive than to ask simply if it was old. Instances showing an even more obvious difference in the degree of suggestiveness could easily be found. Now, where the difference is obvious, no difficulty, theoretically, needs arise; but difficulty might occur if there were a difference that is not obvious. And nothing is easier than to pass from a subjective- direction to an objective-direction leading question without a suspicion that in doing so one is possibly employing the less reliable form of a question. Of course, it is not obvious a priori which (if either) of the two question forms is, e.g., the more reliable; but it is this very fact, combined with the practice of asking leading questions in either form, which makes it important to compare the influence of the two forms upon the answers.

There is another element in the form of a question which has not hitherto been investigated. This element is the article. Does it make any difference to the answer to the question "Did you see a Zeppelin?" if the question is altered to "Did you see the Zeppelin?" This difference is not as trivial as it may perhaps seem. The question with the definite article certainly seems to be more 'implicative' than the question with the indefinite article, and consequently, the small amount of verbal change in passing from one to the other may be connected with considerable changes in the character of the answers. Further, the two questions may be considered loosely typical of questions with vaguely defined and explicitly defined content respectively, since it is generally assumed that the latter form of the question is relatively 'implicative.'

In the present experiment, then, an attempt has been made to investigate (1) the influence of the direction (subjective or objective) of the question upon answers, and (2) the influence of articles upon answers. In addition, several question forms were arranged so that the influence of the negative upon answers might be made clear; and finally, two question forms not connected with the above points were included in the experiment. The latter was 'incomplete disjunction' and the 'implicative' question forms.

2. The Question Forms Investigated in this Experiment

The following eight types of questions have been investigated in the present experiment. Under certain conditions, they would all be considered leading questions. It will be noticed that the first four of them (A, B, C, D) are subjective-direction, and the last four (W, X, Y, Z) objective-direction questions. At the same time, only two subjective-direction questions (A, C) have precise correspondents among the objective-direction questions (W, X).

Reference letter of types. The question forms (direction)

A (subjective) Did you see a...?

B (subjective) Did you see the...? C (subjective) Didn't you see a...? D (subjective) Didn't you see the...? (objective) Was there a...?

X (objective) Wasn't there a...?

Y (objective) Was there a K, m or n...?" Z (objective) Was there a K, m...?

If these types of questions be compared with the types given in Lipmann's classifications, it will be seen that the types marked A, B, and W would be classified in Lipmann's scheme as Yes-No questions; that is, assuming that subjective-direction questions are to be included in Lipmann's classification. It will be seen also that the types C, D, and X, would be classified in Lipmann's scheme as Yes questions. Y is Lipmann's incomplete disjunction question and Z is his implicative question. It is obviously difficult, however, to say what question is 'implicative' and what is not. If Binet was right in supposing all questioning to be a forcing of memory, it would seem that all questions are more or less implicative. It is at least reasonable to consider the types marked B and D as implicative, because they contain the definite article; but these would not be considered as such in Lipmann's classification.

3. Description of the Experiment

(a) Observation material and apparatus. Moving pictures were used as material for observation. A number of photographs, which had been taken in rapid succession, were affixed, in the order in which they had been taken, to the outside of a small cylinder, as spokes to the hob of a wheel. By rotating the cylinder, the separate photographs could be exposed in rapid succession. A cinematographic effect was thus produced. About 450 separate photographs went into the making of each moving picture. These pictures will be referred to as films. They are rotated by means of the motor of a memory apparatus which had been adjusted so that they could be fitted to it. The photographs measured approximately one inch by three-quarters of an inch, but they were observed through a magnifying lens which about doubled their size. They were observed from a distance of about six inches.

Five films were employed in the experiment. These will be designated F0, F1, F2, F3, F4.

FO need not be described at all, as it was used as a preliminary film only. It represented a practical joke.

F1 gave a representation of conjuring tricks performed by one of two men. The men appeared, first of all, to be in a restaurant, and one of them seemed to be giving orders for refreshments to the other. In the course of the film, a hat and a cigar were made to disappear, and a tea service suddenly appeared from nowhere and as suddenly vanished.

F2 showed Marble Arch, London, in the background. In front of it was a part of Oxford Street along which various kinds of vehicles and a number of pedestrians passed in both directions.

F3 showed what appeared to be the main street of a fair-sized country town in England and had as its central incident the yoking of horses to a coach which stood outside an inn.

F4 depicted a practical joke played by a girl and two boys on a stout elderly man. The man was asleep in a basket chair on a lawn, and the girl was hosing the garden. The boys came up and induced the girl to turn the hose upon the sleeping man, after which they poured a bath of water over him.

(b) Subjects. Fifty-six subjects took part in the experiment, twenty-one women and thirty-five men. With the exception of three men and three women, they were all university graduates or undergraduates. From the point of view of social standing and intellectual development, the subjects thus constituted a fairly homogeneous group, or, if a distinction be made on the basis of sex, two homogeneous groups.

(c) Procedure. The time adopted for reeling off each film once was from 25" to 28"; that is, each photograph was exposed about 1/18". The reason for the adoption of this constant rate was that with it, the incidents appeared more life-like than with any other. If it was increased, objects began to blur; while if it was decreased, the film tended to show gaps and jerks.

At the beginning of the experiment, the subject was shown the preliminary film (F0) and was asked to give an account of it. It was explained that this was not a part of the experiment proper but was merely intended to indicate its general character. The preliminary film was shown several times to each subject so that the conditions of the experiment might become familiar and adjustments might take place.

The subjects could not be informed concerning the chief aim of the experiment, as is obvious, e.g., from the relation between subjective-direction and objective-direction questions. In no instance was the object of the experiment subjected. After the preliminary film had been shown, the subject was instructed as follows. "I will show you another, and I want you, after you have seen it, to tell me everything that you can remember of it." Another film was then shown. After its exposure, the subject dictated his report, which was taken down verbatim. He was allowed to continue until he ceased spontaneously. No questions were asked here, whatever the gaps or additions the reports might contain.

The film was as a rule then shown again, after which the subject reported additions to, or corrections to, his first report. Sometimes it was shown a third time, and in rare instances a fourth.

Variations in the number of exposures depended upon the character of the films and the differences between subjects. The principle determining the number of exposures in the case of any subject was that a certain grasp of the film was necessary before the previously constructed questionnaire concerning it could be put. It thus resulted that some subjects required more exposure to a film than others and that most subjects required more exposure to certain films than to other films. It had to be determined roughly by the character of any report whether or not the subject had a sufficient grasp of the film to allow for detailed questions concerning it without further exposure.

The degree of knowledge of the film required from the subject before he was questioned was determined by the character of the questions and the purpose of the experiment. The aim of the experiment necessitated the elaboration, prior to the experiment, of a number of questions about the scenes depicted in the films, these questions being arranged in the different forms which were to be investigated. If a certain knowledge of the films was lacking, at least some of the prearranged questions could not be asked. Thus, one film (F4) contained a bath as a fairly central object, and one of the prearranged questions concerned the position of this object at a certain time. This film was relatively easy, and consequently, only one exposure to it was generally given before the questions were asked. One subject, however, did not mention a bath in his first report of this film, and it seemed evident that he had not seen it. Hence, to make the bath question possible for this subject, the film had to be shown to him a second time. And similarly in other cases.

When it appeared that a subject had acquired a requisite grasp of a film, a series of prearranged questions with regard to it were asked. The subject's answers were taken down verbatim, together with any spontaneous remarks he made, and the attempt was generally made to obtain introspections.

All questions were asked in as even tone as possible, and an attempt was made to reduce suggestiveness from the tone of voice to a minimum.

The time taken for going through each film (report and questionnaire) was generally about one hour (each subject was taken separately). As a rule, one film was taken in one sitting, but in certain cases, two were taken. There were twenty-one women, and each saw only two films. The men saw various numbers. Twenty-five saw four each. Three saw only one each, and the remainder saw three each. These numbers (of the films) are exclusive of the preliminary film. The paper then describes the questionnaire. It is very involved and inclusion of it here would not appropriate; it would have added two times again as many pages!

APPENDIX A.

DEVELOPING TECHNICAL SKILLS

I usually write in the third person (e.g. we, us, they, them) but in this appendix and the next one I am going to write in the first person (e.g., I, me). These two areas are important and personal to my success, so I feel this approach is more from-the-heart - a better way to communicate this content. Also, while I provide suggestions for resources, solutions and references, I have no affiliation with any of them and you should not assume that anything I offer is necessarily best for your needs.

So, why develop technical skills? Remember these four general concepts:

1. Every technical lead or trail begins and ends with one or more humans.
2. Understand the whole picture, interview for information within the context of the technologies relevant to your investigation.
3. Assemble the relevant compliance and legal backdrop (see Appendix B).
4. Understand technology relevant to your domain, experience, and future purposes.

What does this all mean? In sum, the technologies center around digital data that is in use. The data will either be at rest or in motion and it will be manipulated by applications along the way. So, the path starts with a human, follows this path, and winds up back with a human. This path may happen in many sequential paths and/or in parallel and in various permutations. The ability to piece everything together is paramount for a factual understanding that is as complete and thorough as possible. This is the primary tenet of what to learn. The purpose of the investigation, and thus an interview, will follow this breadcrumb trail accordingly.

With rare exception, every person you interview will leverage technology as a major part of their personal and professional life. As well, the "human" may be an IT professional, a technical support engineer, a computer forensics examiner, or any other person in a technical vertical that helps you put the pieces together.

The level and depth of the technical understanding are guided by the context and issues in the investigation. Often, a higher-level understanding of technology will allow you to communicate lower-level questions to those who have more technical depth and expertise in a given vertical. It is then up to you to manage the investigation and assemble these facts into a relevant whole.

However, the technical topics do not fit this "path" so neatly. It may require a patchwork of topics. There are many options. What follows is very thorough coverage that should get you well on your way.

General Learning vs. Certificates vs. Boot camp vs. Degree

Technical training can come in many forms. I generally bucket them into four categories: General Learning, Certificates, Boot camps, and Degrees. These each go in order of commitment. I am going to take them our of order below as I personally believe certification is a best, first option. However, that is a personal decision and one, as always, you should explore for yourself.

General Learning

While I believe certification is the best option, I cannot stress enough how general learning is so important to staying on top of technology. Certain technical areas (such as artificial intelligence, quantum computing, etc.) move at a very fast pace and it is difficult for certificate programs, boot camps and degree programs to keep up. As you become immersed in various areas of technology, you will find Internet searches and use of generative artificial intelligence (such as ChatGPT) to play a big role in your quest.

There are, though, some fantastic online resources (at the time of the writing of this book) that are available generally. I will include links and a quote from their websites.

Coursera

https://www.coursera.org/

"Start, switch, or advance your career with more than 5,400 courses, Professional Certificates, and degrees from world-class universities and companies."

Udemy

https://www.udemy.com/

"Choose from 213,000 online video courses with new additions published every month."

Udacity

https://www.udacity.com/

"Udacity's proven playbook is globally scalable, addressing the widespread digital talent shortages that impact growth, productivity, and innovation. We collaborate with enterprises and highly motivated individuals to design a tailored talent transformation journey enabled by our Digital Competency Platform"

Boot camps

Boot camps can be expensive but are a great way to get a fast, deep immersion in a specific area. They often run for one to two months, full time and cost in the tens of thousands. These should be researched thoroughly first, though. They were once very hot but their relevance has been refined in recent years.

Degree Programs

Degree programs are a big decision and not something that can possibly be covered in the scope of this book. I am sure I am not telling anything you do not already know but a degree will cover one topic very well and may leave others excluded. For example, a degree in computer science may be perfect if you wish to pursue a career in software engineering but may leave out important areas of information technology (IT). Conversely, a degree in IT may cover device, network and cloud technology but may leave out important security topics that are often crucial to an investigation. It is my opinion that our quest may require a more finely-grained learning path. However, if you have done your research, and you believe the commitment is justified, then more power to you.

Certification

Personally, again, I think it makes more sense to start with the certification as a middle ground to learn. The certification proves to others that you have a specific, objectively-tested capability around one or more areas tailored to your purposes. One reason I have certifications is to prove to myself that I am competitive in a given area; it is part of my ethical philosophy to ensure I am properly educated.

Below I include most technical areas that are likely to be relevant for your quest as an investigative interviewer. I will keep it brief with the name of the certification or educational resource. This should not be considered an exhaustive list.

IT generally

Information technology (IT) is a very broad topic that covers devices such as desktop and laptop computers, smart devices (tablets and smart phones), networks, cloud infrastructure and possibly software solutions. Some programs will teach you how to fix problems with the result of employment in a service role such as a help desk or as a IT administrator. Research these topics with this in mind:

https://www.comptia.org/certifications

https://learn.microsoft.com/en-us/certifications/browse/?resource_type=certification#infrastructure

Security/Forensics

This area considers very deep technical analysis typically into hardware devices, hard drives, and evidence at the bits and bytes level. Certifications in this area tend to be crucial if you are starting out or if you plan to be called as an expert witness to defend your findings.This area is quite competitive, sometimes requires a private investigator's license and former or existing law enforcement personnel are common:

https://www.giac.org/

https://www.isc2.org/Certifications

https://www.iacis.com/certification/

https://www.isfce.com/certification.htm

https://www.autopsy.com/

https://www.kali.org/

Vendor specific

Many programs are open source, free or agnostic as to the underlying commercial tools that are offered. However, some educational and certification programs are offered by providers who sell tools to investigate or assess. The upside is that they often come with ample documentation, training and support. This can be very attractive. The downside is that there is what is called vendor lock-in where you will be stuck with what they have to offer. Many practitioners use more than one tool given that no one tool does everything or does it well. So, proceed with an open mind an talk with professionals in the field for further guidance:

https://www.opentext.com/learning-services/certification
https://training.magnetforensics.com/w/
https://www.exterro.com/forensic-toolkit

Applications

There are thousands of commonly used applications, all of which may integrate with many others. Your investigation may lead you through these applications as information and evidence make their way through the digital ecosystem.

Many will become obsolete and many will appear on the horizon. Search for certifications, formal training, and other learning resources for the application (or hire someone who can do this). Here is a smattering:

- Microsoft: Windows Operating System, Office 365, Email
- Mac Operating System
- Google: Gmail, Drive
- Social media, OSINT
- Open Worldwide Application Security Project (OWASP)
- Security Software Development Life cycle (SSDLC)
- Oracle
- SAP
- Salesforce

Auditing

If you are an auditor, the two primary audit associations who maintain certifications, networking, training and similar are below:

https://www.isaca.org/credentialing/certifications
https://www.theiia.org/en/certifications/

Privacy

There is one primary, ubiquitous association for privacy (below). Their certifications are considered, at the time of publication, to be highly sought after and respected:

https://iapp.org/certify/

Conclusion

Do your own research! Ask colleagues, stay up to date. This is a fast-paced, moving target type of area. It will be necessary to understand what you know and don't know and how to rope in relevant technical professionals to flesh out the details. Prioritize and determine the necessary granularity of each component part based on the magnitude, complexity, and budget of your investigation.

APPENDIX B.

DEVELOPING LEGAL SKILLS

In this chapter, we will visit the value of understanding the law and how to pick up these skills. Obviously, I cannot teach you the law here. The amount of information and its applicability would encompass its own series of books. However, I can offer you various resources to include how much time you may need to invest. I am not trying to turn you into a lawyer either. Practice of law requires a license - practicing law without a license is a crime!

This chapter will focus on two overarching topics:

- The law and its general application.
- Compliance and regulations.

Law of General Applicability

There are certain legal topics that are potentially always relevant or that may help you understand other laws or regulations. This is precisely what lawyers are taught. I am an attorney in California and have been for over 20 years. However, my primary motivation in becoming an attorney was not to practice law, it was to become a better investigator and, hence, a better investigative interviewer. I am also a licensed private investigator.

As others hire me as a private investigator, the client knows that I understand the law. When I am out researching and talking to people (as an investigative interviewer), they know that I can pick up on evidence that is potentially relevant and I can continue to dig deeper as I investigate. As I have stated earlier in this book, as an investigative interviewer, you may not have a chance to visit with a person you are speaking with again, so you want as much useful information as you can get in your first contact.

The point is that I have the same legal eyes and ears an attorney does so others know I will not likely miss vital information and evidence. This is one reason why attorneys tend to do well as investigators. It is my belief that there are certain basic legal topics that will give you the requisite breadth of knowledge for most matters and contexts. I'll start with the topics that attorneys learn and how those may or may not be relevant to you as the investigative interviewer. That is the whole point of this chapter.

Depending on how you count the topics, and which jurisdiction you are in, there are between twelve to fourteen topics taught in law schools and tested on bar exams. They are:

1. Constitutional Law
2. Criminal Law and Procedure (some count these as two subjects)
3. Civil Procedure
4. Evidence
5. Real Estate (or Property) Law
6. Contract Law
7. Tort Law
8. Corporations
9. Wills and Trusts (some count these as two subjects)
10. Remedies
11. Community Property
12. Professional Responsibility

The first seven are topics covered on what is called the multi-state bar exam (or MBE) and they are considered more important for general applicability. The remaining five topics are more focused. It is in the seven areas that I think it is a great idea to have working knowledge. Here's why (in no particular order):

Tort law

This is an area that contains the most civil causes (as opposed to criminal) of action that will be brought. Personal injury, defamation, product liability, and interference with business opportunities are examples. In fact, most civil litigation occurs in tort law and those cases are futile without strong facts to support them - facts that are uncovered during investigations and with use of superior interviewing skills.

Here are some educational offerings you can choose to visit (with links and brief description from the website):

Coursera (https://www.coursera.org/learn/american-law)

"Tort law governs how people may sue each other civilly (as opposed to criminally) in order to receive compensation for harms or injuries other people caused them. In this module, Professor Allen will explore the goals of tort law through a historic case. She will address what makes tort law distinct and issues surrounding negligence and liability."

UC San Diego Division of Extended Studies (https://extendedstudies.ucsd.edu/courses-and-programs/tort-law)

"A tort is a civil wrong which is remedied by compensation to the injured party. You will learn what constitutes a tort in this course, including intentional acts and negligent acts such as personal injury and what is the appropriate course of action when someone has been harmed."

The Mass Tort Institute (https://www.masstortinstitute.com/mass-tort-academy/)

"The Mass Tort Institute is an education and training company founded by attorney, CPA, and mass tort business practitioner Terry Dunken. Terry's successes and setbacks in the mass tort industry have given him key insight into working with legal vendors, co-counsel, defense attorneys, and other important players to resolve legal claims for thousands of injured victims. Our mission is to equip legal professionals with the tools they need to successfully resolve legal claims against some of the largest corporations in the world."

Contract law

The bulk of the remaining areas where civil causes of action are found is in contract. Was there a breach of contract? Are there issues of misrepresentation or mistake that may have impacted contract formation? Was a contract formed at all? Are there defenses to a breach of contract? Was a breach of contract a major or minor one? Your ability to flesh out these issues is vital.

Here are some educational offerings you can choose to visit (with links and brief description from the website):

UC San Diego Division of Extended Studies (https://extendedstudies.ucsd.edu/courses-and-programs/contract-law)

"Contract law permeates the entire field of civil practice. This course provides the student with both the theory of contracts and the practical skills needed in contract law. Instruction presents interesting and significant court cases for discussion, emphasizing a practical approach to understanding contracts. Topics include all major areas of contracts, including offer, acceptance, consideration, statute of frauds, third-party beneficiaries, performance, breach of contract and damages."

Lorman Education Services (https://www.lorman.com/contract-law-training)

"Lawyers and paralegals have a responsibility to keep their skills current through ongoing continuing education. If your area of practice covers business and contract law, you can benefit from online training at Lorman Education Services. Experienced legal professionals, many of whom work at top national firms and other prestigious organizations, develop our courses. They're also based on the most recent updates to state and federal regulations. Recent courses have included: Practical Considerations and Concerns in Construction Contract Law; Managing Government Construction Contract Changes; Troublesome Contract Clauses and Their Solutions; And more."

Coursera (https://www.coursera.org/learn/contracts-1)

"American Contract Law I (along with its sister course Contracts II) provides a comprehensive overview of contract law in the United States. The course covers most of the key concepts found in a first year law school class. Each lecture is based on one or more common-law cases, integrating legal doctrines with policy discussions. The course also covers key sections from the Uniform Commercial Code (UCC), which governs the sale of goods."

By the end of the course, the learner should be able to understand:

Formation: how a valid and enforceable contract is created, including concepts such as offer, acceptance, consideration, and promissory estoppel."

The University of Texas at Austin (https://professionaled.utexas.edu/contract-law-specialist-certificate-program)

"Having a paralegal with an in-depth understanding of contract law can be very useful to attorneys during the drafting and litigation stages of a case involving an alleged contract breach. The Contract Law Specialist Certificate Program introduces you to the range of issues and processes that are involved when entering an enforcing contract. Learn from real-world cases to build a better understanding of contract drafting, enforcement as well as defenses and remedies for breaches."

Criminal law (and procedure)

This is one of the most recognizable topics to a lay audience. This spans theft, assault and battery, murder, rape, robbery, child molestation, and many others. Understanding the elements and defenses to each crime better enables understanding what evidence is necessary.

Very often, the intent is the most difficult to prove and much of the evidence gathering will be done by investigators and, in particular, the interviewer. People rarely confess to crimes, so a properly conducted interview might extract information from a suspect/defendant that can only come from an interview. Awareness of the probability of risk is a key issue with intent. Your interview may be the only time and place where this type of information can be fleshed out.

Here are some educational offerings you can choose to visit (with links and brief description from the website):

UC San Diego Division of Extended Studies (https://extendedstudies.ucsd.edu/courses-and-programs/criminal-law-and-procedure)

"Criminal Law and Procedure is a survey course covering the elements of many typical offenses in California and in other states. Some of these offenses include drug offenses, robbery, rape (and other sex offenses), burglary, murder, arson, and driving under the influence. You will be introduced to concepts in criminal law that will be illustrated with examples from actual cases. In addition, criminal procedure will be covered including: the prohibition against unreasonable searches; interrogation and confession; the right to counsel and confront witnesses; and the right to be free from cruel and unusual punishment."

U.S. Career Institute (https://www.uscareerinstitute.edu/online-criminal-justice-school/courses)

"Learn everything you need to know to start a new career as a Criminal Justice Specialist. In this online criminal justice program, you'll start by learning about career opportunities in the industry and then develop a foundation in the psychology of crime and victimization. You'll discover the elements of investigations, crime scenes, and criminal law that show you how a Criminal Justice Specialist fits into each piece of the law enforcement picture."

Penn Foster (https://www.pennfoster.edu/programs/legal)

"If you want to pursue a career in criminal justice, take the first steps with one of Penn Foster's online criminal justice and legal training programs. These affordable programs are all offered online and can be taken at your own pace. From accredited degree programs to career diplomas and certificates, you can find the criminal justice or legal program that is right for you."

Liberty University (https://www.liberty.edu/online/government/bachelors/certificate/criminal-justice/)

"Our online Criminal Justice Certificate provides foundational training in key aspects of the criminal justice system. A certificate can help you be better prepared for certification or promotion opportunities. Throughout this program, you can hone the oral and written communication skills vital to success in both professional and personal settings."

Evidence

What makes information relevant so that it can become evidence? What are the exclusionary rules, such as hearsay? Is evidence admissible at all? Is the evidence authenticated and reliable? Are there any privileges such as attorney-client or physician-patient? Being armed with this information is critical for those who are involved in an investigation. Your ability to address these issues during the investigation can be very helpful to a legal team.

Here are some educational offerings you can choose to visit (with links and brief description from the website):

UC San Diego Division of Extended Studies (https://extendedstudies.ucsd.edu/courses-and-programs/evidence-law)

"Be introduced to the study of the law of evidence. The material covered in the class presents practical applications of the rules of evidence, primarily referring to the California Evidence Code and the Federal Rules of Evidence. Instruction highlights areas that are especially relevant to the paralegal practice."

The National Judicial College (https://www.judges.org/courses/fundamentals-of-evidence-web-based/)

"his course is designed to provide you with a practical framework for ruling on evidence. You will be introduced to the principles of the Federal Rules of Evidence with a focus on using the rules to decide evidentiary issues. This course will benefit judges without law degrees who are looking for a better understanding of evidence as well as judges with law degrees who are looking for a refresher."

National Paralegal College (https://nationalparalegal.edu/Evidence.aspx)

"This course presents a survey of the most relevant and most important rules of evidence. Although an in depth knowledge of the rules of evidence is most important for a litigation attorney, a paralegal should also have a basic understanding of what types of evidence are admissible in court in order to be able to focus a pre-trial investigation in a manner that is likely to lead to the acquisition of admissible evidence. This course will focus on the Federal Rules of Evidence but will also note comparative state laws from time to time when they differ from the federal rules. Important areas of evidence law that the course will focus on include relevancy, character evidence, impeachment of witnesses, hearsay and the original document rule."

Constitutional law

This is probably the most important inasmuch as it spans so many fundamental topics. And, there is a lot of overlap with criminal procedure such as search and seizure and the right against self-incrimination. Equal protection and due process are ripe for issues related to investigations. Other constitutional law topics may be a bit more esoteric (e.g. interstate commerce, freedom of religion, etc.) but a solid grounding in understanding the Constitution is always worth the effort.

Here is an educational offerings you can choose to visit (with links and brief description from the website):

Coursera (https://www.coursera.org/learn/american-law)

"The study of constitutional law is among the most exciting parts of the law because it provides for the structure and functioning of the U.S. government. In this module, Dean Ruger will address the document itself, how it has been applied over time, the history of the document, and what makes it unique. The structure of the U.S. government as a government of limited, separated powers will be explored along with the important individual rights the Constitution provides and how the U.S. Constitution compares to others around the world."

Civil Procedure

Civil procedure is perhaps not as relevant to the investigation as some of the other topics but it is very helpful to understand what phase a case may be in such as jurisdiction and venue, pretrial procedures, motions, trial, verdicts/judgments, and appeals. The type of evidence and amount of evidence necessary often turns on the phase of the matter as it winds its way through the court docket.

Here are some educational offerings you can choose to visit (with links and brief description from the website):

UC San Diego Division of Extended Studies (https://extendedstudies.ucsd.edu/courses-and-programs/civil-litigation-i)

"Receive a thorough overview of the civil litigation process. The first of a two course series, instruction will cover the procedures for preparing a case for trial, from prelawsuit investigation through trial. The focus is on procedures within state courts with some discussion of federal court procedure also. The course describes the paralegal's function during the litigation process and ways in which paralegals can expand their level of responsibility."

Coursera (https://www.coursera.org/lecture/american-law/civil-procedure-part-1-3kNtP)

"In this module, Professor Wolff will introduce us to some of the major issues in civil procedure law. Civil procedure is the study of the rules of court that must be followed by the judge and parties in civil cases (as opposed to criminal cases – criminal procedure is a whole other area of the law, but law students learn civil procedure first because it gives the structure of typical trials). The essence of a law school civil procedure course is the study of the Federal Rules of Civil Procedure. A copy of these is linked in the syllabus for you to scan. The rules tell you how to file a lawsuit and how the court must function while it is considering a lawsuit. Professor Wolff will introduce you to the doctrinal area of procedure and will highlight some of the major modern issues in procedure law."

Property

Of the MBE topics, this may be the least relevant unless you are involved in a dispute over real property, such as landlord/tenant disputes, possessory interests, and easements. However, many courses teach this at a higher level to include personal property and intellectual property. Where there are issues of ownership, right to possess or control, etc., information and evidence obtained in an investigation will be key.

Here are some educational offerings you can choose to visit (with links and brief description from the website):

UC San Diego Division of Extended Studies (https://extendedstudies.ucsd.edu/courses-and-programs/real-property-law)

"Discover the most commonly encountered problems when preparing and drafting documents for real estate transactions and learn how to solve them. Fundamental principles of real estate law, including ownership, sale, leasing, financing, & government regulation are surveyed. Instruction covers practical and procedural tasks involved in California real property law, including drafting and reviewing basic documents such as deeds, promissory notes, deeds of trust, purchase and sale agreements, and residential and commercial leases. Remedies available to secured parties in real estate financing transactions, title insurance, escrow, foreclosure, and landlord-tenant relationships are also covered."

Coursera (https://www.coursera.org/learn/american-law)

"Property law governs the relationship between individuals and things, known as property. In this module, Professor Balganesh will explore the differences between property and tort and contract law and about several specific examples of property law in action: adverse possession, landlord/tenant, and licenses. You will learn about what makes U.S. property law distinct - its origins in common law, imprint of legal realism, and pragmatism."

Remaining Five Topics

The other five topics can be quite relevant depending on the area. For example, corporate governance, a topic common in compliance, is very useful. A course on corporate law (as taught in law school) would be a very good idea. If one is investigating a family law case, a course on community property law would be excellent. A course in wills and trusts would be helpful for probate and estate disputes. But I am not going to boil the ocean here. If you feel you could make good use of these other topics, I would encourage you to research them.

The path to obtaining the requisite knowledge in these seven areas has many paths, and each has its own pros and cons.

Jurisdoctor ("J.D." or "Law Degree")

One option is to go to law school. In my humble opinion, this is more likely a net loss unless you have a very good reason for doing so and you have a well-informed basis for the time commitment and expense. It is three years full-time (or four years part-time) and the cost is approaching $200,000 with tuition and considering living expenses and books, etc., at the time of the writing of this book. If you just want to understand the law to be a more effective investigator, I think this path may be a diminishing return. In other words, I am not sure I would have made the same decision to go to law school knowing what I know now.

There are many programs. Some are larger schools approved by the American Bar Association (ABA) and others are smaller schools, typically less expensive, with state-level approval/accreditation (which may be necessary to sit for the bar exam in that state). Some are online and some cater to certain verticals (e.g. tax, technology, intellectual property, etc.).

There is so much more that can be said here, and it is important to understand your reasons for going to law school. If you plan to practice law, an ABA-approved school will probably be necessary to work for larger law firms. Beyond that, I am not sure the cost and commitment is worth it. Consider what you want to do and how much you think you need to know.

One common and reputable resource for learning more about ABA schools is the U.S. News and World Report rankings. See:

https://www.usnews.com/best-graduate-schools/top-law-schools/law-rankings.

Otherwise, Internet searches are likely to be your best option.

Master of Studies in Law (MSL) Degree

Another path is to get a degree in a master's program called the Master of Studies in Law (MSL) Degree, which is touted as a degree for non-lawyers (or for those who do not want to become a lawyer). Pepperdine University, Northwestern University, and the University of Southern California Schools of Law each have such a program. They are online and do not require graduate tests such as the LSAT or GRE, though a bachelor's degree is usually required. Whether the master's program covers the seven topics we mentioned above is a matter for further exploration and relevance, i.e. it may be that the master's program does not cover the seven areas but the program may take a different approach that may be acceptable for your purposes. Internet searches will better flesh out options as there are many.

Legal Certificate Programs

This option requires less commitment than a master's or J.D. and some tend to be focused on a specific area of law (though some are more general). More general certificate programs are called Legal Studies Certificates while others are for specific areas such as:

- Law and technology
- Environment, energy, and natural resources
- Media
- International trade
- Human resources
- Tribal law
- Intellectual property
- Constitutional law
- Entrepreneurship
- Estate planning
- State and local taxation

The University of Southern California (USC) has programs in the following areas:

- Business Law Certificate
- Compliance Certificate
- Financial Compliance Certificate
- Health Care Compliance Certificate
- Human Resources Law and Compliance Certificate
- Entertainment Law and Industry Certificate
- Privacy Law and Cybersecurity Certificate

Note that USC's program is not the only one and I have no affiliation with the university or the program. USC's program is one option and there may be many others and with other types of certificates. Internet searches and other research will be your best bet inspired by the information you are getting here.

Other Options

There may be other courses that offer single topics in law, such as criminal law, evidence, contract law, etc. The same tenet applies that having the peripheral legal vision of the seven topics will provide roughly what lawyers have. Whether you choose to get a J.D., a master's degree, or education in a single topic, is up to you. Degrees and certificate programs will let others know you have the requisite skill and knowledge. Less formal options may provide certificates or they will just prove your value which will come out in your work (which may be enough).

Unauthorized Practice of Law

There is one very important issue to be aware of as you develop legal knowledge. Every state has a law called the unauthorized practice of law (UPL) and it is a crime. Unless you are a licensed attorney in the jurisdiction where you "practice," you cannot represent others in court and you cannot give legal advice, whether for money or not. Giving legal advice means making legal conclusions or decisions based on facts. So, if you tell me that you hit someone in self-defense and I tell you that you committed a battery but that it was justified as in self-defense, I am making legal conclusions about your factual situation - that is the practice of law. Unless one is licensed as an attorney in that state, that person is committing a crime.

It is legal to tell someone what the law is, e.g. the definition, you cannot do more. So, in your reports or communications to others, you should indicate that you are not authorized to practice law and that any conclusions or assertions about the applicability of the law to facts should be made by someone that is authorized to provide legal advice, i.e. an attorney.

Compliance and Regulation

The primary challenge with this area is how does one define "compliance" or "regulation"? For example, the terms "risk," "governance," and "compliance" are considered distinct yet their definitions, in my humble opinion, simply overlap.

There is no hard answer and the terms can become ambiguous, and even confusing. However, there are some approaches that should cover most cases, at least with regard to what I have seen as most common. Note also that there is a strong overlap with the technical certifications and content in the previous appendix. As always, use your intuition, common sense, and best judgment when considering options in your research.

The primary issue with compliance and regulation is whether some person or entity has been non-compliant or engaged in an activity prohibited by law or regulations.

Highly Regulated Verticals

Highly regulated industries such as financial services, healthcare, pharmaceutical, energy and government will have their own compliance and regulatory regimes. Each of these verticals (and others) are splintered in their own way with varying degrees of depth. It makes much more sense to discuss certifications, associations, and learning paths with those in the vertical or domain than for me to give you advice here.

General Compliance and Regulation

Those areas of compliance and regulation that are not necessarily devoted to a vertical, like finance or healthcare, will involve one or more permutations of the following areas:

Regulatory

This is about as broad as you can get and considers all laws and regulations that a person or entity needs to comply with. Given how highly varied this can be, you should consult an appropriate professional, such as an accountant, a lawyer, or a tax professional. I hate to sound like I am passing on answering this more specifically and directly, but I would be irresponsible in asserting otherwise.

Compliance

Compliance tends to fall into a number of common categories. These are some important areas that are more common. I have included the area of compliance / regulation followed by websites with brief descriptions:

Government

Association of Government Accountants (https://www.agacgfm.org/home.aspx)

"Advance. Grow. Accelerate.

AGA is the association that connects and empowers financial related professionals who support government, from financial management to IT, human resources, cybersecurity and more, to advance good government initiatives, grow their expertise and accelerate their careers.

We connect and empower professionals to help them:

Advance sound financial practices, accountability, transparency and excellence in government

Grow, learn, excel and engage through a network of like-minded professionals and leaders

Accelerate professional careers through learning opportunities and the opportunity to earn a unique credential - the Certified Government Financial Manager, the only credential developed solely with the government financial professional in mind. Through thought leadership, certification, and national and chapter educational events, AGA remains at the forefront of emerging issues and innovation — driving excellence and transparency in government accountability."

American Society of Military Comptrollers (https://asmconline.org/)

"ASMC Mission: To promote thought leadership, professional development, nd ethical behavior in all aspects of defense financial management.

ASMC Vision: ASMC will be the premier organization bringing people together in advancing thought leadership, professionalism, and ethics within the national security financial management community."

American Public Works Association (https://www.apwa.net/)

"The American Public Works Association (APWA) serves professionals in all aspects of public works—a fact that sets it apart from other organizations and makes it an effective voice of public works throughout North America. With a worldwide membership more than 30,000 strong, APWA includes not only personnel from local, county, state/province, and federal agencies, but also private sector personnel who supply products and services to those professionals. Membership in APWA is open to any individual, agency, or corporation with an interest in public works and infrastructure issues."

Senior Executives Association (SEA) (https://www.seniorexecs.org/)

"MISSION: The Senior Executives Association is a professional association that: Promotes good government initiatives and practices that empower senior executives and federal leaders for mission success; Advocates for legislation and policies in the interests of the federal career senior executive service; Facilitates networking opportunities for, and with, federal governmental leaders; Connects current, rising, and aspiring leaders with continuous professional development opportunities."

Energy

The Energy Professionals Association (https://www.tepausa.org/)

"Established in 2005, The Energy Professionals Association (TEPA) is a not-for-profit organization of professionals dedicated to advancing competitive energy markets across the country. TEPA is a membership-based association that provides professional development, advocacy, certification program, and access to a network of respected industry leaders.

Our association operates as a self- governing organization to ensure that market participants conduct themselves in a professional manner, have access to accurate information and opportunities to collaborate with other industry professionals. We strive to provide our members with suggested best practices for transacting in the marketplace all while working with the best interest of the end user in mind.

Working with a TEPA member ensures that end users are working with a company dedicated to providing quality service. TEPA members who have achieved our Energy Management Professional (EMP) designation have demonstrated acumen with regards to energy markets, procurement strategies and best practices."

Financial Services

Association for Financial Professionals (https://www.afponline.org/)

"As the certifying body in treasury and finance, the Association for Financial Professionals (AFP) established and administers the Certified Treasury Professional (CTP) and Certified Corporate Financial Planning and Analysis Professional (FPAC) credentials, setting the standard of excellence in the profession globally. AFP's mission is to drive the future of finance and treasury and develop the leaders of tomorrow through certification, training, and the premier event for corporate treasury and finance."

Society of FSP (https://national.societyoffsp.org/)

"The Society of Financial Service Professionals is a multidisciplinary community of accomplished professionals whose common purpose is to deliver the highest level of ethical service to their clients. In an environment promoting professional development and ethical conduct we welcome as regular members qualified professionals who hold one of the following credentials: AEP®, CASL®, CEBS®, CFA, CFP®, ChFC®, CIMA, CLF®, CLU®, CPA, CPCU®, CTFA®, Enrolled Actuary, JD, MBA, MSFS, MSM, Masters/PhD in Financial Services, REBC®, RHU®, RICP®"

National Society of Compliance Professionals (https://www.nscp.org)

"The National Society of Compliance Professionals is a nonprofit, membership organization dedicated to serving and supporting the compliance professional in the financial services industry. NSCP is "For Compliance, By Compliance." NSCP membership provides financial services compliance professionals with a wide range of compliance resources, continuing education to further their knowledge and specialized skills, and regulatory involvement through representation of compliance interests. NSCP members have access to a diverse community of compliance professionals who willingly share their knowledge and expertise."

Institute of Financial Operations (https://myfinancialops.org)

"The Institute of Financial Operations is a non-profit, membership-based professional association serving the financial operations ecosystem, with a particular focus on the accounts payable discipline. The Institute grew out of the merger of four associations: International Accounts Payable Professionals (IAPP), International Accounts Receivable Professionals (IARP), the National Association of Purchasing and Payables (NAPP), and The Association for Work Process Improvement (TAWPI). Based in Orlando, FL, with affiliates in the U.S., and Canada, The Institute serves as a global voice, chief advocate, recognized authority, acknowledged leader, and principal educator for people in financial operations. The Institute has a community of nearly 50,000, which includes over 9,000 members and customers, and an additional 41,000 financial operations professionals. The Institute's members have access to benefits and leading-edge resources such as a dynamic content-rich website, educational and networking events, online educational offerings, certification and certificate programs, career resources, and volunteer opportunities."

Risk Management

Risk involves the balance of threat, or probability of harm, balanced against the cost to mitigate the harm. Note that it is not possible to remove all risk, so approaches focus on the "risk appetite" that one can justify. Many major schools offer courses in this area but it depends, as usual, on the area of application. Many focus on insurance and financial risk while others focus on health and safety while others cover enterprise risk.

Professional Risk Managers' International Association (https://www.prmia.org/)

"Established in 2002 by a volunteer group of risk industry professionals, our mission is to provide an open forum for the development and promotion of the risk profession. To accomplish this mission, the objectives are: To be a leader of industry opinion and a proponent for the risk management profession; Drive the integration of practice and theory and certify the credentials of professional risk managers; Connect practitioners, researchers, students and others interested in the field of risk management; Be global in focus, promoting cross-cultural ethical standards, serving emerging as well as more developed markets; and Work with other professional associations in furtherance of our mission."

RIMS—the risk management society (https://www.rims.org/)

"RIMS, the risk management society®, empowers risk professionals to make the world safer, more secure, and more sustainable. Through networking, professional development, certification, advocacy, and research, RIMS and its 80 chapters serves more than 200,000 risk practitioners and business leaders from over 75 countries. Founded in 1950, the Society publishes the award-winning Risk Management Magazine and produces RISKWORLD®, the largest annual gathering of global risk professionals. RIMS embraces diversity, equity and inclusion and welcomes all risk professionals to connect and learn, explore the online Risk Knowledge library, tune into the RIMScast podcast series, and engage via social media. To learn more, visit www.RIMS.org.."

The Risk Management Association (https://www.rmahq.org/)

"For more than 100 years, RMA has been laser focused on one thing: helping its members in the world's financial institutions better understand and address risk. As a trusted partner, RMA has weathered the many economic ups and downs of the last century alongside its members, which now number 1,600+ financial institutions of all sizes, from multi-nationals to local community banks. These institutions are represented by over 41,000 individual RMA members located throughout North America, Europe, Australia, and Asia.

Our members rely on us to keep them abreast of important industry trends and prepare them to face new challenges head-on. Our sound risk management principles are developed for members, by members, and help to build safer, stronger financial institutions, impacting local communities and the global economy.

Our Mission: To advance enterprise-wide risk management in the financial services industry through education, products, and community. "

Global Association of Risk Professionals (https://www.garp.org/)

"GARP is the leading professional association for risk managers, dedicated to the advancement of the profession through education, research, and the promotion of best practices.

RISK CERTIFICATION AND EDUCATION

GARP's Financial Risk Manager (FRM®) Certification and Sustainability and Climate Risk (SCR®) Certificate are the leading global designations for risk managers. We also offer Continuing Professional Development (CPD) opportunities, and courses in Foundations of Financial Risk (FFR®) and Financial Risk and Regulation (FRR®) to strengthen organizational risk awareness."

The Institute of Risk Management (https://www.theirm.org/)

"The IRM is the leading professional body for Enterprise Risk Management. We help build excellence in risk management to improve the way organisations work. The Institute of Risk Management (IRM) is the leading body for professional Enterprise Risk Management (ERM). We provide globally recognised qualifications and training, publish research and guidance and set professional standards. We are a not-for-profit organisation, with IRM members working in all industries, across several risk disciplines and in all sectors around the world. IRM's qualifications have been developed by internationally recognised academics and industry practitioners. They give you the theory, tools and techniques to manage risk, maximise opportunities and protect your organisation."

Governance, Risk, and Compliance

This is a very common area which is, as you can tell from its name, a set of overlapping and synergistic topics.

The Association of Governance, Risk and Compliance (AGRC) (https://a-grc.org/)

"AGRC is a place for knowledge-exchange, professional networking and idea incubation. The Governance, Risk and Compliance (GRC) requirements are evolving at a pace that makes it challenging for professionals to follow and manage all aspects of this complex ecosystem. Our certification programs aim to raise the standards of ethics and integrity in the world of compliance, governance and risk, whilst boosting our industry's knowledge and understanding of new technologies."

International Association of Risk and Compliance Professionals (IARCP) (https://www.risk-compliance-association.com/Welcome.html)

"We invite you to connect with a global community of experts working in risk and compliance management, to explore new career avenues, and most of all, to acquire lifelong skills. Join us. Stay current. Read our weekly newsletter with news, alerts, challenges, and opportunities. Get certified and provide independent evidence that you are an expert. Become a CRCMP. This is one of the most recognized designations in risk management and compliance. There are

CRCMPs in 57 countries. Companies and organizations around the world consider the CRCMP a preferred certificate."

Compliance Next (https://www.navexglobal.com/compliancenext/)

"Compliance Next is both an online community and a state of mind for modern, innovative compliance professionals. It's a place to network with peers without organizational boundaries. Learn and share best practices. And be part of the next generation of compliance program innovation."

Privacy

In the present digital age, privacy compliance has become one of the top areas of risk. There are laws in the European Union that are very strict and most other countries have developed or are developing similar laws. Many states have also passed laws that are widely applicable and with strong penalties.

International Association of Privacy Professionals (https://iapp.org/)

"Your comprehensive global information privacy community and resource The International Association of Privacy Professionals (IAPP) is a resource for professionals who want to develop and advance their careers by helping their organizations successfully manage these risks and protect their data. In fact, we're the world's largest and most comprehensive global information privacy community."

Global Association of Data Protection Professionals GADPPRO (https://gadppro.org/)

"The Global Association of Data Protection Professionals (GADPPRO) is the only global network association (NGO) that brings together professionals active in the space of privacy, data protection, security, trust, compliance, ethics and integrity with the ultimate aim of converging and standardising global best practices for the same by drafting, negotiating and acceptance based on a unique member consultation approval mechanism."

Ethics

Ethics is another very broad and ambiguous term but it does have a specific meaning in the compliance community. However, there is the potential depending on the domain or vertical that could suggest another set of rules and regulations.

Association for Practical and Professional Ethics (https://www.appe-ethics.org/)

"About APPE: Established in 1991, the Association for Practical and Professional Ethics (APPE) is a non-profit 501(c)(3) membership organization dedicated to advancing scholarship, education, and practice in practical and professional ethics. APPE fosters moral reasoning skill development, works to promote ethical conduct in all sectors of our daily lives, nurtures the next generation of ethical leaders, and seeks to advance civil public discourse on diverse ethical issues."

Society for Business Ethics (https://sbeonline.org/)

"Who We Are: We are a diverse, global group of students, scholars and business professionals from all disciplines, interested in the research, discussion, teaching and application of ethical business practices."

Society of Corporate Compliance & Ethics (https://www.corporatecompliance.org/)

"Society of Corporate Compliance and Ethics® (SCCE®) is a member-based association with 7,000+ compliance and ethics members worldwide. SCCE was founded in 2004 by Health Care Compliance Association® (HCCA®) to support compliance and ethics professionals across all industries. The vision of SCCE is to be the pre-eminent compliance and ethics association promoting lasting success and integrity of organizations worldwide. In 2011, SCCE incorporated with our founding organization to form Society of Corporate Compliance and Ethics & Health Care Compliance Association (SCCE & HCCA).

Certification through the Compliance Certification Board (CCB)® — Certification options include Certified Compliance & Ethics Professional (CCEP)®, Certified Compliance & Ethics Professional–International (CCEP-I)®, and Certified Compliance & Ethics Professional Fellowship (CCEP-F)®."

Ethics & Compliance Initiative (https://www.ethics.org/)

"The Ethics & Compliance Initiative (ECI) empowers organizations to build and sustain High Quality Ethics & Compliance Programs (HQPs). ECI provides leading ethics and compliance research and best practices, networking opportunities and certification to its membership, which represents more than 450 organizations across all industries. ECI is comprised of three nonprofit organizations: the Ethics Research Center, the Ethics & Compliance Association and the Ethics & Compliance Certification Institute.

CERTIFICATION: The Ethics & Compliance Certification Institute (ECCI) is the certification arm of ECI. It represents a strong rigor in education and certification for ethics and compliance practitioners and represents the evolution of the certification program (formerly conducted by the ECA's Foundation). Certification helps prepare practitioners to deliver a new level of excellence to their organizations."

Healthcare

Many major universities have training programs or certifications in HR compliance. These include but are not limited to Cornell, University of Southern California, Drexel University, etc.

American College of Healthcare Executives (https://www.ache.org)

"For over 85 years, the American College of Healthcare Executives (ACHE) has focused on one mission—advancing leaders and the field of healthcare leadership excellence. We are the professional home to more than 48,000 healthcare executives who are committed to integrity, lifelong learning, leadership and diversity and inclusion."

The American Association of Healthcare Administrative Management (https://aaham.org)

"The American Association of Healthcare Administrative Management (AAHAM) is the premier professional organization in healthcare administrative management. Your one-stop resource center for information, education and advocacy in the areas of reimbursement, admitting and registration, data management, medical records, patient relations and so much more."

American Health Information Management Association (https://www.ahima.org)

"The American Health Information Management Association (AHIMA) is the leading voice and authority in health information, wherever it is found. Our people work at the intersection of healthcare, technology, and business."

Association for Healthcare Administrative Professionals (https://www.ahcap.org/)

"AHCAP is a not-for-profit healthcare association dedicated to executive assistants, administrative assistants, and other professionals who support our nation's healthcare leaders. By supporting healthcare leaders, we support the industry - and strive to enhance the healthcare experience on every level. We are proud to be the only national association dedicated exclusively to administrative excellence in healthcare."

Notes

[←1]
https://onlinemasteroflegalstudies.com/resources/legal-certificates/
[←2]
https://online.usc.edu/news/best-online-law-certificates-non-lawyers/
[←3]
https://gdpr-info.eu/
[←4]
https://oag.ca.gov/privacy/ccpa

www.ingramcontent.com/pod-product-compliance
Lightning Source LLC
LaVergne TN
LVHW011521200926
848484LV00001B/104
* 9 7 8 0 9 1 1 9 8 3 0 5 0 *